THE
Busy Moms' GUIDE TO
Indie Publishing

ANGELA CASTILLO
& JAMIE FOLEY

Copyright © 2018 Fayette Press

10 Digit ISBN: 0998207837
13 Digit ISBN: 978-0998207834
AISN: B07BR96VTX

Published in Bastrop, Texas

This novel is a work of fiction. Names, characters, places, and incidents are either used fictitiously or are products of the author's imagination. All characters are fictional, and any similarity to persons living or dead is coincidental.

Printed in the United States of America

Glossary

DEDICATION   1

CHAPTER 1: THE GOOD, THE BAD, & THE UGLY OF INDIE PUBLISHING
- Why indie publishing is so awesome   4
  - The pros of going indie   4
  - The cons of going indie   8
- Maybe going indie is biting off more than I can chew...   12

CHAPTER 2: FUNDRAISING (OTHER THAN BAKE SALES)
- Ideas for easy moolah   19
- Crowdfunding   21
- Don't give in to vanity   23
- Priorities and patience   26

CHAPTER 3: HOW TO MAKE A BAD BOOK COVER, GUARANTEED
- Just becuase you *can* doesn't mean you *should*   28
- How to make a cringe-inducing cover (or not)   29
- Our recommended artists   33
- Custom illustrations   33
- Staging a photoshoot   35
- What your designer should deliver   37

CHAPTER 4: FROM PIXELS TO INK: PAPERBACKS & PRINTING
- Should I publish my book in paperback?   40
- How much will my paperback cost to produce?   41
- Which printer should I choose?   44
- Pictures and color and pop-ups, oh my   48
- Pirates and booty (yarrr!)   51
- CreateSpace tutorials   52

CHAPTER 5: **EBOOK FORMATTING AND THE KINDLE MONSTER**
- Formatting your book for Kindle — 61
- How to upload your book to Kindle Direct Publishing — 64
- Pricing strategies — 65
- Amazon's sneaky fee: the download downlow — 66
- Should I enter the KDP Select program or 'go wide?' — 68
- Formatting for all other ebooks: the universal EPUB — 71

CHAPTER 6: **AUDIOBOOKS**
- Recording your own audiobooks — 73
- ACX to the rescue — 75
- Choosing a narrator — 77
- Selecting music — 79
- Audiobook covers — 79

CHAPTER 7: **BELLS & WHISTLES: CATEGORIES, KEYWORDS, BLURBS, AND MORE**
- Front matter: Down in front! — 82
- Back matter: Junk in the trunk — 82
- Should I name my chapters? — 85
- Don't be shy—it's time for your biography! — 85
- To pen name or not to pen name — 86
- Choosing categories — 87
- Setting up your Amazon Author Page — 88
- Keywords & tags — 89
- A few thoughts on book descriptions/back cover copy — 91

CHAPTER 8: **NOT-FOR-PROFIT BOOKS**
- So, when's your next concert? — 93
- Creating an affordable not-for-profit book — 95
- Pointers for common types of not-for-profit books — 97

CHAPTER 9: PRE-MARKETING: PREPARING FOR LAUNCH

- A note on time and money   101
- Pre-launch marketing   103
- Reviews   106
- Marketing to the great beyond   109

CHAPTER 10: MARKETING PLATFORMS: FOUNDATIONS FOR YOUR INDIE CAREER   112

- Base building: Places to set up your platform   113
  - Your author website & blog   114
  - Social media   116
  - Email newsletters   118
- Building relationships & spreading the word   120
  - Local bookstores   121
  - Libraries   122
  - Book fairs/events   122
  - Forums   123

SOURCES   126

OTHER BUSY MOM'S GUIDES

- *The Busy Mom's Guide to Novel Marketing*   128
- *The Busy Mom's Guide to Writing*   129

50 WEBSITES EVERY AUTHOR SHOULD KNOW ABOUT   131

- *Free .PDF download with newsletter sign up*

ABOUT THE AUTHORS & THEIR FICTION   132

TO OUR *husbands.*

ALL THE WORDS WE COULD EVER WRITE COULD
NEVER EXPRESS OUR LOVE AND GRATITUDE.

Chapter 1

THE GOOD, THE BAD, AND THE UGLY
OF INDIE PUBLISHING

> "The idea that an artist needed to suffer to do her best work was a conceit of the young and inexperienced. The happier she grew, the better she wrote."
>
> — Dean Koontz, *Lightning*

So, you've got a manuscript you want to indie publish, eh? Maybe you just finished your first book (despite the sticky-fingered toddler on your lap) and don't want to tangle with a literary agent, publishing house, or the financial stress of it all. Or maybe you've tried and ended up with enough rejection letters to keep your kid's crayons happy for years. You're not alone.

Or perhaps you have already released books with a publisher, but your royalties aren't what you'd hoped… and you're looking to supplement your income.

It's possible you have no idea whether you should indie publish or try for a traditional contract, but you saw this book and thought, "At last, *someone* who understands what I'm going through!"

We *do* understand! We have children of our own, and budgets, grocery lists, messy houses, and all those other things that have to somehow get accomplished between morning and night. And yet, we squeeze in time to write as well! We have realized that writing is an important part of our lives... a part we can't just put on hold until after our children are grown and gone.

And—let's face it—you can probably find most of what's written here somewhere out in the interwebs, stuffed in between all kinds of misinformation. But why spend all the days and weeks and months when we've saved you the trouble? Momma don't got time for that! (Okay, grammatical errors noted. Yes, we are real writers. From Texas.)

This book isn't about *how* to write—or how to find time to—since we covered that in the first book in this series, *The Busy Mom's Guide to Writing*. What you will find here is how to turn that stack of papers or file on your hard drive into a smooth, glossy book with your dream cover, the perfect teaser blurb, and sprinkles on top. *Without* pulling your hair out or breaking the bank.

WHY INDIE PUBLISHING IS SO AWESOME

As you can tell from the title, we have written this book mostly for those of you who have already decided to go indie (otherwise known as *independent publishing* or *self-publishing*), but if you are still on the fence regarding traditional publishing versus indie publishing, here are some points to consider.

THE PROS OF GOING INDIE

- **Once your manuscript is ready, you can publish at any time.** You don't have to wait years to find an agent, then more time for your book to be sold to a publisher, then for the publisher

Am I ready?

Here's a handy checklist to help you know if you are ready to indie publish your book to sell. (If you aren't planning to write your book for profit, you might want to zoom over to Chapter 8: Not-for-Profit Books.) If you answer 'no' to any of these, you may want to check out *The Busy Mom's Guide to Writing* before starting your indie publishing journey.

1. My book has been finished and completely typed up on a word-processing program like Microsoft Word or Google Docs.

2. I have a professional cover with an awesome, clearly readable title. (Check out Chapter 3: How to Make a Bad Book Cover, Guaranteed for clarification).

3. My book has gone through a extensive editing process by professional editors, including content editing or critiquing from a reliable critique group, beta-reading, and copy-editing for spelling, punctuation and grammar issues.

to edit, go through legalities, marketing, and finally launch your book on their schedule. Not having to wait is especially helpful if you write sequels and want to get them out quickly.

- **You don't have any deadlines** (except those you create for yourself, and you *should* try to have goals). This is especially good for moms with younger children, since, well, life happens. It's wonderful to be able to put writing on hold for soccer season, the last two months of pregnancy, or when the whole family catches the flu. Plenty of moms have been published by a traditional agency, but almost all of them will tell you that meeting deadlines can be a stressful roller coaster.

- **You keep *all* the money.** Well, most of it—every sales platform, such as Amazon, will keep a portion. But you will make a high percentage off of every sale, and continue to make money every month without having to wait the years some traditionally published authors have to endure before they see a royalty check.

  Indies also don't need to pay a literary agent around 15% of their royalties, which all of the large traditional publishers require.

- **Your books are always the center of attention.** Think about it: publishing companies have new contracts constantly in the works. If they get a book that becomes more successful than yours, what are they going to put time and energy into? The new shiny book.

  However, if you publish for yourself, you will constantly be working to promote and get your work out there. This means your series can continue to make money for years.

- **You can publish whatever kind of book you want.** If you want to mix up ten different genres in a glorious kaleidoscopic mishmash, there's no one to tell you, "Nope." This is actually what caused both Angela and Jamie to decide to go indie

> "I'm definitely an indie girl. Basically, I like having the ability to control the process and make my own decisions. I am also passionate about releasing what I've written instead of waiting for approvals or rejections from publishers. **I guess I like being my own boss.** I have no regrets. I think I've accepted my flaws along the way, too. It's a learning process."
>
> — *Traci Vanderbush*

in the first place. Angela couldn't find a single agent in the United States of America who would accept queries for a middle-grade/sci-fi/Christian/allegorical/fantasy *(The Toby the Trilby series)*, and Jamie didn't even try to find a publisher to take her clean young adult/urban fantasy/dystopian *(The Sentinel Trilogy)*. So they decided to publish their own books the way they wanted to, thank you very much.

The great thing about indie publishing? *No one tells you what to do.* You are free to share your art exactly the way you want to. Does this mean you shouldn't have critiques or edits? Of course you should! But ultimately, you choose what and how you want to share your writing.

- **No gatekeepers.** Your manuscript won't have a massive

slush pile to make it through, or editors who pass on your work because it's not trendy enough (or perfectly aligned with their current tastes) to make the grade. But you should have a team of people to read through your work and help you know when it's ready. More on that later.

THE CONS OF GOING INDIE

- **All upfront costs are paid by you.** As moms, we know you may not have an extra dollar to spare for your projects. But if you think about it, there's usually something you can cut back

THE BEAUTY PAGEANT

Traditional publishing gatekeepers are like beauty pageant judges. They don't help you develop your craft or encourage you along—they only judge the final product before them. If you decide to go traditional, you'll need at least one editor and a good critique group to help your book get to the best place it can possibly be so it can pass through the panel of judges and ultimately reach your readers.

If you decide to go the indie route, your book will also require a team to support and perfect it—like a pageant contestant needs a coach, personal trainer, makeup artist, choreographer, et cetera. So while you won't have to worry about getting a winning score from a judge before you can have the green light to publish your book, you will need all the elements to create a winning book… or *it won't sell.* Future chapters will go into detail about how to select editors, cover designers, and formatters to ensure your book reaches its fullest potential.

on. I mean, do we really need Netflix *and* Hulu every month?

How much would you expect to invest when starting a small business? Because that's what you're doing when you become an indie author. You need training and supplies and people to ensure that your business will be successful and profitable. So the costs of indie publishing can get pretty high. Most indies we know have spent anywhere from $50-$3,000 (or even more) to produce a single book. We have an entire chapter dedicated to estimating costs and helping you figure out how to raise funds, so don't forget to check out Chapter Two: Fundraising (Other Than Bake Sales).

- **You do all your own marketing.** Indies don't have a publishing company to help them with marketing. But the truth is, even traditional authors have to do most of their book's marketing on their own in this modern day of social media. So if you decide to go traditional later on down the road, it's good to have a platform established and marketing skills polished. There's a lot to learn about marketing, which we'll discuss in Chapter Nine: Pre-Marketing (and the next book in this series, *The Busy Mom's Guide to Book Marketing*).

- **Genre matters.** Even though you can self-publish whatever you want, if you are planning to make a go of this for profit (and let's face it, most of us want to make some money from writing), then genre really does make a difference. Some genres have readers who fly through stacks of books every month and will buy every similar book they can get their hands on (such as romances, mysteries, and thrillers). Other genres such as middle grade, children's fiction, and regional non-fiction depend more on local sales to really take off.

We aren't saying it's impossible to make sales with certain genres, but your strategies may be different depending on the type of book that you write—and your expectations may be different, too.

- **Blood, sweat, and tears.** As a mom, your time is precious, but books will not produce or sell themselves. If you are going indie, you will have to devote a certain block of time and money to assemble your team of professionals, create your book in various formats, and market it.

But guess what? We're here to help you with all the details!

WHAT ABOUT HYBRID AUTHORS? CAN I HAVE MY INDIE CAKE AND EAT IT, TOO?

A hybrid author is someone who is both traditionally *and* indie published. More and more successful, established traditional authors are indie publishing on the side.

Why? Because they make a higher profit margin on their indie books. Unfortunately, traditional authors just aren't making as much money as they did several years ago. This could be due to a number of factors, including the rise of ebooks, video games, and Netflix (which, honestly, we love too).

Jamie recommends a hybrid marketing strategy for anyone lucky enough to land a traditional contract with a *large* publishing house. This strategy has the highest earning potential for the author because it results in the large audiences of fans (through the publisher's additional marketing efforts) while maintaining the author's highest royalty percentage (through indie earnings).

Sounds like a pretty sweet deal, huh? Just bear in mind that large publishers like the Big 5 (HarperCollins, Macmillan Publishers, Penguin Random House, Hachette Book Group, and Simon & Schuster) and others can be restrictive in their contracts, so your indie publishing options may be limited unless you have a negotiating rockstar of an agent.

This is why some authors like Jamie decided to indie publish first before seeking a traditional contract. More and more agents are becoming friendly toward indie authors, and so are publishers—indies already know the ropes of the industry, and we can prove it with sales numbers and positive reviews of our writing.

IF I GO INDIE, AM I GOING TO HAVE TO SPEND THOUSANDS OF DOLLARS JUST TO GET PAPERBACK COPIES OF MY BOOK?

This is the question we are asked most often so we wanted to address it right here: no. You can produce a paperback book for a very reasonable amount, especially if you just want to make copies for family and friends and/or produce a few copies to sell at a local shop.

But if you produce a book for cheap, expect it to appear cheap. If you're looking to make a career out of writing, you need to produce a quality product that people will be happy to pay for—and that will require an investment.

We love making our money stretch as far as possible (you should see Angela's mad couponing skills), so one of our primary goals with this book is to help you produce the best possible book at the best price.

THE UGLY: THE VANITY TRAP

You might have already found companies that say they will produce your book for you, design the covers, and even list your book in 'prominent book catalogs.' For this privilege they will charge you, oh, $2,000 or more. And guess what? You even get to have ten copies of your book for family and friends!

These companies are called vanity presses, and we will never, ever, ever, *ever* recommend you use them. We'd rather give our kids Kool-Aid right before bed on a school night. We'll talk about this in more detail in Chapter 2.

MAYBE GOING INDIE IS BITING OFF MORE THAN I CAN CHEW...

Yes, indie publishing can be a huge commitment, like starting any other career or small business. If you don't treat it that way, you won't see much profit.

Indie publishing is like making fruitcake: you get out of it what you put in. If you pay $1.00 for a book cover and half a sandwich for editing, don't expect your book to become a bestseller. You probably have better chances of winning the lottery.

This is a calling. It's a passion. If you want to find success, expect to dedicate several hours a week to making it happen—like a part-time job or even a full-time career. And if you dive in with excitement and discipline and willingness to learn, it could be one of the most satisfying adventures you ever take.

If this seems daunting—especially as a mom—remember that you can take a break whenever you need to. It's one of the best pros of becoming an indie author: you're your own boss.

It is our hope that through this book, you won't have to learn lessons the hard way like we did. We strive to answer your most burning questions—and the ones that the Internet can't seem to make up its mind about. Let us solidify the gray areas into black and white for you, so you can make the best decision for yourself and your family.

And if you decide to indie publish, let us give you our favorite tips and tools for your best chance at success. We'll cheer you on along the way.

QUESTIONS

1. What is publishing my book worth to me—and to my family—in terms of money and time?
2. How much time can I budget each day to learn more about publishing and marketing, and to move forward with this process?
3. Who can I go to for encouragement and support along this journey? (One answer is the Busy Moms Facebook group, accessible via our Patreon page!)

Chapter 2

FUNDRAISING
(OTHER THAN BAKE SALES)

*"'Starving artist' is acceptable at age 20,
suspect at age 40, and problematical
at age 60."*

— Robert Genn

If you are in the 49% of Americans who live paycheck to paycheck,* you're probably wondering how much your book is going to cost to produce, and if you can afford to put it together without taking on a second (or third) job. Which would eat up all your writing time anyway.

It's hard to pinpoint how much *your* project will cost to put together, since everyone's book is going to be different. For example, a contemporary women's fiction novella will probably be less expensive to produce than a children's picture book with hand-painted illustrations.

So let's figure out a rough idea of how much your book will cost to produce, and then we'll help you work out how to raise the moolah for it... hopefully without your children having to live on ramen for the next two years.

Please note: everyone's budget is going to be different. Plenty of authors get their book out for almost nothing—but scrimping and skimping is normally not the best plan, especially when you're selling a product to strangers who will then rate that product. Your book's reviews on Amazon will play a large role in its success over time.

Here are some of the common costs associated with producing your own book:

Editing: $200-$3,000+. Editing costs will depend on how much your writing skills have been refined through critique groups and practice, the types of editors you choose, and how many different editors you hire. Editors' rates can vary wildly depending on their qualifications—a college student might ask for $50 for a proofreading, while a well-known editor might charge $500. Also, most editors charge by the word or page, so a 30,000-word novella will cost less than an 110,000-word fantasy novel.

Here are some estimated ranges for the different types of editing:

- Developmental/Substantive: $100-$1,500
- Copy/Line edits: $150-$2,000
- Proofing: $50-$500

If you're just getting started, remember that you might need multiple rounds of developmental edits to make a draft really shine. Please don't spend a fortune on an editor until your book has gone through inexpensive developmental work first, like beta readers and/or a critique group. You will almost certainly lose money and waste your time.

Now that Jamie took time to learn the craft (it took about five years), she's gathered awesome alpha and beta reader teams (you can find out more about finding beta readers in Book 1, *The Busy Mom's Guide to Writing*) and discovered editors who enjoy working for her at a discount. Because of this, she doesn't spend more than $1,000 on edits for a first book in a new series, and only about $300 for books 2, 3, and so on.

Angela goes a different route. She uses an extensive critique group called Scribophile for developmental edits, then sends her books to beta readers, then finally turns her book over to copy-editors, which are generally much less expensive than substantive (or developmental) editors. So she spends less than $200 for editing in every aspect. But keep in mind, Angela has spent 28 years studying the craft of writing, reading books, and listening to seminars. We aren't saying 28 years of study is necessary for good writing, but classes and craft books do help the writing process a lot.

Cover design: $25-$2,000+. This should be your top priority if you plan on selling books. If you want to make sales, *people do judge books by their covers!* Especially now that competition is higher than ever. Check out Chapter 3 for more detail on cover design.

Paperback & ebook formatting: Free-$500. If you're good with computers, you might be able to handle the formatting yourself. But we're not going to lie: it's an absolute pain in the neck to get started.

The Amazon KDP (Kindle) website has an automatic formatter that can turn your Microsoft Word document into a Kindle book for free. But it will probably look like the monster in your kid's closet chewed up your book and spat it out. KDP does have a free ebook preview tool, but

Sometimes Kindle's free formatting tool can create errors that a professional would need to fix, anyway. Angela had a problem with that—and Amazon flagged her book page saying that people had reported formatting issues. Yikes! She turned to a professional formatter to re-format the book.

ebooks will appear differently on different devices. So it's best to make sure you have it formatted right in the first place.Other ebook platforms like Nook have their own free tools on their websites for you to use, but most of them are known for being painstaking and buggy.

Paperback formatting is also a challenge. Going through the approvals process with your printer (which will probably be CreateSpace if you're going indie) can last weeks and rack up costly proof orders if you're trying to work out all the bugs yourself.

We recommend trying one of the formatting packages at Book Baby. It costs around $300 - $500 for their ebook and paperback formatting without having them print a bunch of starter paperbacks for you. They have a nifty quote calculator on their website at www.bookbaby.com.

Several other services, including individual businesses, will format ebooks for a price. If you decide to go with one of these services, we highly recommend you compare prices and check reviews before you hire them. If someone is offering to format your 500-page manuscript for ten bucks, yeah, you might need to reconsider.

If you want to give it a go yourself, check out CreateSpace. They have a free paperback template download for Microsoft Word with page numbers, headers, title pages and everything else already installed. This is what Angela does, but it still takes time and headaches to figure out, so be warned.

You can also find a publishing program to help you with your formatting needs. Vellum is one of these programs, though it only works with Mac computers. Scrivener is a formatting software you can purchase for either Mac or PC and will also help if you want to convert a file from one format to another (e.g. MOBI to PDF). But like every other formatting option, there's a learning curve.

Or if you happen to be a wiz with HTML and CSS, you can use Adobe Dreamweaver or another website design program for Kindle formatting. Likewise, graphic designers familiar with Adobe InDesign can format their own books for paperback. Jamie has a professional background and education in this area, so she does her own formatting in this regard. We'll go into more detail on formatting in Chapters 4 (for paperback formatting) and Chapter 5 (for Kindle formatting).

ISBN: Free-$125. Every print book (paperback, hardcover, etc.) requires an ISBN, which is related to the barcode on the back. It handles the book's information for bookstores and libraries, like its list price, dimensions, subtitle, back cover copy, and more. Check out Chapter 4: Paperback Formatting Without Pulling Your Hair Out for more info regarding ISBNs.

> Ebooks do not require ISBNs. If you publish through Amazon Kindle (KDP), they will create a special number for your Kindle ebook for free called an ASIN. Yep. You heard that right. Finally something is free!

Paperback copies: $2-$20 per book. One of the fondest dreams of most authors is to hold their finished product in their hands. Thanks to several wonderful online companies called POD (Print On Demand) printers, you can order as many copies of your book as you would like and pay the same cost per book, no matter how many copies you order. In the olden days, you would have to order a large number of books at a time, which is why traditional publishers ruled with print runs. Not so anymore!

There are several POD companies to choose from, such as CreateSpace, IngramSpark, Lulu, and Book Baby. In addition to binding services, these companies also offer other paid services such as editing, formatting, and cover design.

Branding & promotional costs. There are also costs associated with your author brand, such as your website and business cards. But we won't go into marketing costs like promo sites and giveaways, since we cover those in our third book, *The Busy Mom's Guide to Novel Marketing*.

Now, how much should you spend on each of these components? We know authors who have spent anywhere from a few hundred dollars (either they had mad skills in graphic design and formatting or traded services with people—Angela's books have all cost less than $400 each to produce) up to thousands and thousands of dollars. It really depends on what you are looking for.

IDEAS FOR EASY MOOLAH

After you have worked through this book, you should formulate a basic idea of how much it may cost to produce your creation. So how do you raise the money?

Please don't put everything on a credit card with the idea you'll make it all back as soon as your masterpiece is published. While this *could* happen, it's highly unlikely. Most authors have to work for several months to build momentum. And like any new small business, it can take a few years to turn a profit.

Please talk your budget over with your spouse. And again, present realistic expectations. Do they spend money on a hobby or sport? You might present this as budgeting for your hobby. Like we said, there is every possibility you can make a profit with your writing, perhaps even a hefty profit, but it's not guaranteed.

Most of your free time is probably spent wrangling kids and (hopefully!) writing, or maybe working another part-time or full-time job, but here are some ideas to quickly raise at least a portion of the extra cash you will need to self-publish a decent book.

1. **Out with the old.** Go through every room in your house for things to sell. Check for appliances you never use, gifts you unwrapped but never opened, books, gently used clothes, etc. You never know what's hiding under your kid's bed.

2. **Never gonna read that again, anyway.** Check all of your media (like books, DVDs, CDs, etc.) to see if they have any value on Amazon.com. List them for sale on sites like Ebay, Craigslist, or Amazon.

3. **Garage sale.** Ask friends and family if they have unwanted items to contribute to a garage sale to help out with your book fund. Then hold the mother of all garage sales. Have your cutest kid right out front selling bottles of water. Well, maybe not that last part. Or at least give them a cut of the profits.

4. **Crowdfunding.** Start a fundraiser on Kickstarter, GoFundMe, or Indiegogo. Offer signed copies, handmade items that go with your theme, etc. for contributions of higher amounts. We highly recommend you do this *after* the editing and formatting process, so you can give people a realistic time frame to receive their goodies. (See the Crowdfunding section below.)

5. **Coupon.** Angela saves at least $50 a week on groceries and household items with coupons. The Krazy Coupon Lady app is a great place to start. (Save $50-$200 per month.)

6. **App-tastic.** Spend a few hours a week working for an app program like Takl, Uber, or Care.com.

7. **The taste of home.** Make dinner at home instead of eating out for two meals a month. Doing meal prepping for casseroles and soups once a week is a way to save even more money with this method. (Save $30-$200 per month.)

8. **A smart breakfast.** Invest in a self-timed coffee maker and make your own coffee every morning instead of going to Starbucks or another coffee shop. Make muffins or scones and freeze them for breakfasts instead of grabbing pastries at a local bakery. (Save $40-$200 per month.)

9. **Kids don't care if it's gently used.** Buy kids' clothes from thrift stores or consignment shops. Many consignment stores will pay cash or store credit for gently used clothing, toys, baby equipment, and books. Or join a mom swap Facebook page and swap clothes and toys for free.

10. **TV shenanigans.** Cancel your cable service and switch to Netflix, Hulu, or Amazon Prime. Or if you have all three of these, pick one and cancel the other 2, and switch out every month. This one step alone could save you over a hundred dollars a month. Or you can get a Roku stick like Angela for a one-time cost of $30 and watch hundreds of TV shows and movies, including streaming PBS Kids, for free. (Save $30-$200 a month.)

11. **Get crafty.** Cut back on how much you spend on another hobby, such as crafting. Or sell your crafts on a website such as Etsy. This is especially nice if you can think of a craft to tie in with your book. We know crafty mamas who sell dolls that look like their book's characters, handcrafted bookmarks, even crocheted animals like dragons and foxes.

12. **Get creative.** Have other creative skills? Check out sites like Fiverr for online opportunities to make an income from home. Fiverr has a large marketplace for freelancing designers, developers, video editors, musicians, voiceover artists, and yes—writers!

The key to becoming a career indie author is promoting and marketing, so it's a good idea to eventually find a monthly cash flow—no matter how small—that you can put into your book until you start to turn a profit. Even twenty dollars a month can help!

CROWDFUNDING

If you already have a large marketing platform (social media, blog, or newsletter audience), or if you just have a ton of friends or generous family, consider launching a crowdfunding campaign on a website like

Kickstarter, GoFundMe, or Indiegogo. Crowdfunding campaigns have many benefits—like gathering people to help your book across the finish line and raising a few thousand dollars—but running a campaign also takes a *lot* of work.

Browse Indiegogo or Kickstarter and find campaigns similar to what yours would be. Answer these questions about them:

- How much money did they raise? Did they fund (reach 100%) successfully within the time period?
- What kind of rewards did they offer to backers? Can you offer similar rewards at similar price points?
- How much did they invest to make the campaign itself a success? You can get a good idea by whether or not they have a seemingly professional video and/or graphic art.
- How large is their audience? Find them on Facebook and Twitter and see how many likes/follows they have. Audience size may be the strongest indicator of a campaign's success (if a reasonable goal is targeted).

Jamie's friend, Thomas Umstattd of Author Media, has an audio course with some great information if you'd like more details. If you search for *The Ultimate Crowdfunding Course for Authors,* you'll find that, unsurprisingly, the course itself was successfully crowdfunded on Indiegogo.

The course is not free, but if you are seriously considering crowdfunding, Jamie considers this course to be well worth the investment before you begin this particular adventure. The 'Magic Spreadsheet' that's included will estimate how many backers you can expect depending on your audience size, and therefore what a reasonable goal would be for your project.

DON'T GIVE IN TO VANITY

We dusted over this in the previous chapter, but in your quest for a published book, you might have run across what is known as a vanity press, or a subsidy publisher.

They *sound* great. You pay them up front, and they'll take all the hard work of making a book off your hands, by doing all the editing, cover design, and formatting. They might even offer to list your book in catalogues and on Amazon.

But these publishers come with a hefty price. We personally know dozens of authors who have shelled out thousands of dollars to their vanity publishers, only to make a few sales. These publishers pad their packages with extras that sound good, but in the long run will not contribute to many sales.

Please do your research. There are many small companies out there who will offer the same services for a much lower cost than vanity presses and do a better job for you.

Another issue with vanity presses: many of them have had run-ins with the BBB, and we have met authors whose manuscripts have been taken off Amazon and 'held hostage' for years in legal limbo. We know an author who lost control and access to her books for several years because of a company called Winepress. We also know an author who was ruined by Tate Publishing, whose founder and CEO were arrested on charges of embezzlement, extortion and racketeering.* Don't let this happen to you.

A TRAGIC TALE OF VANITY

"My advice to anyone thinking of using a vanity publisher is to run in the opposite direction as quickly as possible. Why am I so against them? One published my very first book and by the time I woke up, they'd taken around four thousand dollars from me.

"And for what? They promised a quality review, which I now believe

my book would have passed even had it been about the importance of baskets on bicycles.

"They left me terrified for days. I received a publicity packet with no idea how to use it, so-called advertising in newspapers and on radio

THE DRAWBACKS OF VANITY PRESSES

Vanity presses can be tempting. These companies know just how to woo excited writers with their fancy packages and promises of becoming a bestseller. But in reality, most of these companies deliver a sub-par product for way too much money. Here are some of the complaints authors have had about vanity presses:

- **Ridiculous prices.** Authors are asked to pay huge up-front costs, and then fleeced for hidden charges later on that weren't part of the original package but are all of a sudden necessary. True publishers will never ask an author for money. (But printers will naturally charge for printing each book you request.)
- **Terrible editing.** Though the company promises professional editing, many authors complain of multiple typos left in their manuscripts. Also, many of these companies will not offer developmental editing, historical or scientific reference checks, and checks for simple things like name changes and timeline discrepancies.
- **Ego-stroking.** These people want money. So even if your book really needs more development and structure to make it a marketable story, they'll tell you it's ready for release in order to collect.
- **Holding books hostage.** Even though the writer is assured they will retain all rights to their books, many have found their books inaccessible because of presses going bankrupt or simply dropping off the grid forever.
- **Delayed/unpaid royalties.** Though companies will assure authors of premium paychecks, sometimes royalties will be less than promised, or even worse, never paid out.

stations—possibly even a radio interview, and the most expensive purchase: $1,200 for a professional edit. The $1,500 cost for helping to find a studio that would make a movie from my book was the eye-opener. I was not so dazzled as to think my first book was movie-worthy.

"'Dazzle' is actually an accurate word for what they do to writers. The company finds new writers with dreams of becoming novelists and—here's the important part—little or no idea of what to do. Then, the company interlaces compliments with, "But you need this, too, if you want your book to sell." They 'sold' me one-year's rights to a website but did nothing to help me with it. A picture of me and one of my books were all that was on it.

When you're passed from person to person, it's because each is 'your assistant' in different departments. They may just sit there and pass the phone back and forth for all I know. The person who initially helped me get started was my coach during the entire 'publishing adventure,' but he stopped taking my calls after I reached the $3,000 mark. And that editor they assigned my book to? As soon as I completed my editing classes and received my certification, I pulled the book off my shelf and was soon mortified. Misspellings, commas, and apostrophes were arbitrarily sprinkled throughout the print. Incomplete sentences abounded along with my favorite: paragraphs consisting of one very, very long sentence.

"Please don't think I was a daffy, scatterbrained person. I was in my fifties and a retired teacher. My husband worked as a correctional officer at a prison. We were not unintelligent. Yet, we were dazzled by the dream this vanity publisher promised to help come true.

"I have since learned from an ex-employee of a different vanity publisher that a true publishing company will never ask you for money. I've been an indie publisher since he sat with me at lunch during a conference and walked me step-by-step through the process. It isn't easy, and I don't know if I'll ever become a best-selling author unless I change my name to James Patterson, but I write for my readers.

"Don't be dazzled by a publisher to the point you forget what you're doing."

— Georgia Florey-Evans, author of the *In Shadow* series

PRIORITIES AND PATIENCE

Publishing a book can take time, so if you need to do it in bits and pieces, that's fine. Remember: you're an indie! No one's forcing you to get it done by a certain date.

Taking more time to practice your writing and hone your skills will be better in the long run, anyway. We understand it's hard to be patient—we are two of the least patient people in the entire world when it comes to getting our writing out there—but trust us, it's better to end up with a quality product than to rush it.

QUESTIONS

1. How much money do I estimate this book will cost?
2. How long will it take to save money for my book?
3. What are some ways I can raise money for my project?

Chapter 3

HOW TO MAKE A
BAD BOOK COVER,
GUARANTEED

"If people don't notice your cover or don't connect with it, the author of the book next to yours will be very grateful."

— David Leonhardt

Whoever said people don't judge books by their covers didn't sell very many books.

Let's face it: anyone who visits Amazon.com is going to be inundated with dozens, perhaps hundreds of covers. Your book needs an eye-catching cover to cause someone to pause and click, or if it's on the shelf in a bookstore, to grab it, turn it over, and read the back.

Not only does a great cover capture the reader's attention, but if it's designed correctly, it will also illustrate what kind of book it is even before the reader has a chance to read the description.

Many bookstores will opt to put fewer items on a shelf so they can place books flat with their covers displayed to passers-by. It's not uncommon for people to purchase a book simply because the cover promised them a wonderful story.

In order to figure out how to make the perfect book cover, you have to learn what *not* to do. A great resource for this is LousyBookCovers.com. Be prepared to spend quite a bit of time on this site; it is very educational and hilarious at the same time. The most important thing to remember: don't let *your* book cover get featured! They say any publicity is good publicity, but we're not so sure.

This is one of the reasons why we *highly* recommend you have a graphic artist put your cover together—preferably one who specializes in book cover design. Unless you have had extensive experience in this specific department, you do not want to do this on your own.

JUST BECAUSE YOU *CAN* DOESN'T MEAN YOU *SHOULD*

Jamie has worked with Photoshop since high school. She's earned a Bachelor's in Arts and Technology. She worked as a graphic artist for twelve years. Did she design her own book covers for *The Sentinel Trilogy*?

Nope.

She hired a professional cover designer and paid top dollar for it. But why would she spend the money if she could do it herself—especially as a penny-pinching busy mom?

Designing a book cover is so much more than just making something nice to look at. It's a precise specialty that involves strategy and experience in that particular area. Covers communicate the book's genre (and even its subgenre) through:

- Imagery
- Font
- Layout
- Color

And more subtle factors that professional cover designers specialize in. There are plenty of graphic designers out there (like Jamie), but the vast majority don't have the experience to create awesome book covers that will effectively communicate genre.

If you wanted an oil painting to hang above your mantle, would you hire a sculptor to do it? If you needed two dozen cupcakes for your kiddo's birthday party, would you ask the sushi chef downtown? Maybe, but you probably wouldn't expect the best possible result. (Sushi cupcakes. Yuck.)

If you're indie publishing with the end goal of making a profit, you need the best possible artwork to represent your hard work and draw people to purchase your book. If you skimp on the cost of everything else, don't sacrifice your cover!

HOW TO MAKE A CRINGE-INDUCING COVER

1. **Choose a random photo from your phone and slap on a random font.** Angela admits—she did this with one of her first books. She found a nature picture by her photographer sister, Cherie Haines. A pretty picture. She put the title and her name on the cover and figured that was that.

   The problem? Her book was a sci-fi/fantasy novella aimed at middle graders. The nature picture had absolutely nothing to do with the book. So unless you're writing about a specific state park and want a picture of your subject matter, it's best to avoid random landscape photos.

   Later on, Angela paid an artist to create a cover with a stock photo. Though it wasn't expensive and certainly won't win any awards, It's much more age-appropriate, speaks to the genre and subject, and kids are much more excited about it when she sells books at local craft booths.

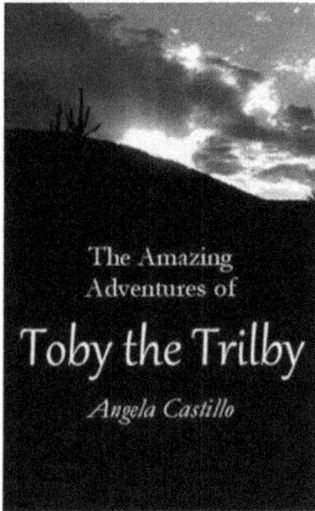

OLD COVER

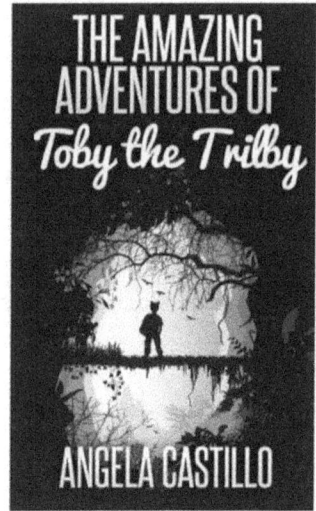

NEW COVER

2. **Choose imagery that has nothing to do with your genre.** One of the easiest ways to see if your planned cover works for your genre is to check out the most popular covers on Amazon.

    For example, if you have a legal thriller set in New York City, you'll want to avoid happy couples frolicking on the cover. If you're planning a sci-fi adventure, you won't want a cowboy galloping somewhere on his horse. Unless that horse is a robot.

3. **Steal a picture from the internet.** While there *are* free pictures on legit stock sites for the taking (like Unsplash.com), you can't just snag a picture from a Google search to use for your cover. We don't want to spend our hard-earned royalties on

lawsuits. Well, *we* don't. Kids go through shoes way too fast.

Even the websites that offer free pictures often have stipulations. They might only allow pictures to be used on websites, for example, but not on merchandise for sale. Or they may only allow a certain number of physical copies to be created. This can also be the case with purchased stock photos, so be aware of the fine print.

Here's another thing to consider about free photos: if you found an awesome photo for free, chances are high that other authors in your genre will also find it and use it for their book.

4. **Use low-quality, grainy photos.** Be careful not to use pictures that are pixelated or too low resolution. People definitely notice—covers with this issue will scream, "Unprofessional!" A pro designer will make sure your book looks great if it's thumbnail-sized or on a giant banner at your book fair. A good rule of thumb is to select photos that are 300 DPI (Dots Per Inch) and/or at least 3,000 pixels wide.

5. **Pick a stock photo that's been used on fifty other covers.** We get it: original photographs don't come cheap. We've run into the same problem countless times.

    But if you're getting a picture from a stock photo website, chances are it's been used for another book cover. Or a dozen others. Jamie's biggest cover pet peeve is the 'girl underwater in a dress' photo that's pretty much its own cliché. There are also several photos of smiling couples that are used for dozens of contemporary romance covers.

    That *can* be okay—a talented graphic designer can do all kinds of things to make a photo unique. But if it's the most popular photo in a category, it has probably been used *a lot*. Try to find an image that fits in your genre but makes your book stand out.

After finding very few pictures that fit a historical novel series, Angela ended up staging her own covers with friends for models. Her covers are absolutely unique and only cost about $250 each, including graphic design, thanks to talented friends.

6. **Make covers for the same series that don't match.** It's absolutely crucial that a reader can see a row of book covers and know at a glance they are all from the same series. On Amazon, you don't want any confusion. Confusion means fewer sales. Every time.

7. **Get your child, sibling, quirky aunt, or enthusiastic friend to design your cover.** Unless they are a professional artist, but you're probably going to have rose-colored glasses when it comes to your family and friends. If you ask someone to make you a cover and it looks awful, it makes for a very awkward situation—and possibly a fractured relationship—when you have to decline.

Amateur artists make amateur covers, and 'almost just right' still doesn't make it work. But something you *can* do with 'fan art' is showcase it on your website or Facebook page. It's a nice way to point out that hey, you do have fans, while saying 'thank you' to the artist. But please don't sacrifice possible sales for the sake of being polite. You've worked too hard on your writing for that!

> "Confusion means fewer sales. Every time."

OUR RECOMMENDED ARTISTS

We highly recommend you don't go cheap on a cover. But there are many talented cover designers out there who can put together a lovely cover for you without breaking the bank.

For affordable cover design, check out Elaina Lee at forthemusedesign.com or Louis Wrift at indigoforest.weebly.com. Angela has worked with both of them on various projects, and had great results for excellent prices. Jamie has a personal friend at Magpie Designs who's a talented cover designer: magpie-designs.weebly.com. We've also heard good things about derangeddoctordesign.com and yocladesigns.com.

SelfPubBookCovers.com is another good option if your budget is tight. You can choose from thousands of pre-made covers, easily customizable with your book title and author name. But again, even though the book covers here are one of a kind, they have been designed with stock photos that are not.

Or, for one of a kind custom designs of the highest caliber, check out Kirk DouPonce at dogeareddesign.com. His covers make us want to weep happy tears. (Check out the covers of Jamie's books in *The Sentinel Trilogy* for examples of his work.) Fiona at fionajaydemedia.com and Seedlings Design Studio at seedlingsonline.com are also reportedly awesome.

CUSTOM ILLUSTRATIONS

If you are looking for illustrations for a fantasy or children's book, check out DeviantArt.com and redbubble.com. Both are great showcases for artists all over the world. Another good place to find artists that work specifically with cover design is upwork.com.

Here are some tips on selecting the right artist for your project:

- **Look through any portfolios they have available,** including other book covers. Check the dates on their works of art and pay attention to the most recent pieces. Artists can improve over time, and their style can change as well.

- **Factor in medium and method.** Are you interested in a flowy watercolor style? Or a computer-designed vector image? Make sure the artist you are considering has portfolio work in the medium you are interested in.

- **Make sure the artwork is cover-friendly.** There needs to be space for a title and your author name without interfering with the rest of the art. It also needs to be vertically-oriented, meaning that it should appear taller than it is wide in order to fit the standard book cover dimensions.

- **Be prepared to spend some real money.** Original cover art can cost anywhere from $100 for an artist who is just beginning to build a portfolio to several thousand dollars.

- **Make sure your artist knows the size your book will be.** Your book's dimensions could be the standard 6 inches wide by 9 inches tall, or many other different sizes when it's printed. Your artist will need to know the dimensions so their art can transfer to that size without compromising the layout.

- **You may have to pay an artist *and* a cover designer.** Not every artist has experience in book cover design, and the last thing you want to do is ruin your beautiful cover with the wrong font or typeset design. Be prepared to pay a cover designer to add your title font and compose your back cover if you are creating a paperback book. Your artist—especially if they are a classical artist like a painter instead of a graphic artist—may not know how to do this.

- **If you want exclusive rights to photos of models in period costumes,** check out periodimages.com. They offer a variety of costumes, models and poses. Not cheap, but worth it if you want authenticity and originality.

Please don't cobble something together if you don't have tremendous experience in graphic design (and plenty of research into what it takes to design a great cover). Your manuscript that you've invested so much into deserves more than that!

STAGING A PHOTOSHOOT

Many indie writers have successfully staged their own photo shoot. It absolutely can be done—Angela did it with her *Texas Women of Spirit* series. But here are some guidelines to hopefully make the process less intimidating.

1. **Pictures don't lie.** If your book is about 17th century England, there's no way your cover model should be wearing an iWatch. Unless the book is about time travel.
2. **Make sure you don't have any visible name-brand items in your picture,** especially a particular vehicle's identifying feature. This is a lawsuit waiting to happen.
3. **Ask around for special props.** You never know what Aunt Ida has in that attic of hers. You might find that exact spinning wheel you need for your *Sleeping Beauty* retelling. (True story. Except my aunt's name is Mary.)
4. **Use a professional photographer.** Check out their portfolio and make sure they do the type of work you need. They might even be able to get you in touch with a model who looks like your main character.
5. **Make sure your backgrounds aren't too busy.** Your graphic design artist might change the background, so make it easy for them to 'cut out' the picture of your model. Make sure the lighting is good and there aren't too many shadows in the picture. Beware of leafy trees scattering the light overhead—that will make your model look splotchy in the photos.
6. **Check local vintage stores for costumes.** The owner might even be willing to lend you the costume for free in exchange for a shout-out on your Facebook page or acknowledgements page, or rent you the costume for a small fee.
7. **If possible, have a few costumes to choose from,** and arrange for a costume fitting with your model before the day of the shoot. This is also a good time to experiment with hair styles,

make-up, etc. Many photographers charge by the hour and you don't want to waste precious daylight/shooting time on wardrobe malfunctions.

8. **Try several different poses in a variety of environments.** Even though you probably have an idea in mind, you might just discover something even more wonderful by accident. It's also a good idea to have a variety of photos for your cover designer to choose from because what looks best in real life isn't always what looks best on a cover layout.

9. **Give your graphic artist your top 5 or 10 photos,** and make sure to let them know if there are more to choose from. Sometimes factors we don't normally consider will contribute to whether or not a picture can be used—like how a certain pose allows for enough room for your title font. Layout can be a tricky business, so the more wiggle room your designer has, the better.

10. **Ensure that your photographer will grant you all rights,** including the ability to put the cover on a product you'll be selling as well as marketing materials. Be clear with your photographer about whether or not they can post photos on their own portfolio, website, or social media. If you're planning on a big cover reveal, displaying the photos ahead of time could ruin it!

11. **Get your model to sign a model release form.** You can find and print these out online. You will probably never need this, but it's always better to be safe than sorry. For minors, you will need their parent to fill out a release form.

12. **If you're planning to have young children on your cover,** have a plan B just in case. Children, no matter how cute, are always unpredictable.

WHAT YOUR DESIGNER SHOULD DELIVER

You won't just need a front cover design from your artist, but the back cover and spine as well.

When the artwork is finished, your designer should deliver the final file in the form of a PDF called a cover spread. It spread should include the front cover, spine, and back cover. It will look a little backwards with the back cover on the left, spine in the middle, and front cover on the right, but that's how it should be. It needs to be in that order so the spread will wrap properly around the book when printed.

Your cover spread should be high-resolution—300 DPI and several thousand pixels wide (the exact width will depend on the dimensions of your book). Your cover designer should have included a 'bleed,' which is a fraction of an inch of extra space outside the edges. The purpose of this is to account for minor misalignment during printing, so a small error on one side will look like a continuation of the artwork instead of a jarring white line.

If you can't find your printer's specifications on their website, contact them for help instead of uploading your artwork without knowing. That will only send you through several rounds of frustrating, time-consuming changes.

SAY THANKS!

Don't forget to thank your cover designer with a mention somewhere in your book. Jamie likes to thank them on the fine print on the back cover and in the acknowledgements. Or you could put a mention near your ISBN and copyright info in the front interior page.

Jamie also sends her artist a signed paperback copy of the final product (the editors get one, too). Of course it's not required for you to do this, but it's surely appreciated! Besides just being a nice thing to do, it's a good idea to maintain a great relationship with your artist for the next book in the series, or the next project altogether.

QUESTIONS

1. How much can I budget for a book cover?
2. What do the bestselling book covers in my genre have in common?
3. Who are some artists, graphic designers, or cover artists I already know who might give me advice during this process?

Chapter 4

FROM PIXELS TO INK:
PAPERBACKS & PRINTING

"A computer does not smell ... if a book is new, it smells great. If a book is old, it smells even better... And it stays with you forever."

— Ray Bradbury

If your children are in school, you've probably had the discussion about how even though homework isn't fun, it has to be done. And your children (if they are like ours) probably answer 'Whyyyyyyyyy?!?"

To most writers, formatting a book is the least fun part. Most of us hate doing it ourselves, farming out the work can be expensive, and for newbies, the entire process can be intimidating. Many writers choose to put this task in the hands of the professionals, and for good reason. Formatting can be quite awful—the process for every type of book is often riddled with meticulous, frustrating IT errors.

But we're indies, right? The whole point of being indie is doing everything ourselves, and many of us simply don't have the $200 or more it takes to shell out for formatting.

So we'll share a few basic tips and tricks, but much depends on the formatting program and printing or publishing service you decide to use.

One of the first questions a prospective self-publisher asks us is, "How can I afford to print out my book?" A decade ago, the only way a writer without the backing of a publishing company could create a book was by using a vanity press or a bindery. Like we mentioned in chapter 2, these companies (which are still around) charge thousands of dollars up front to edit, format, print, and design a cover for your creation.

But we don't have to do that anymore. There are several amazing companies out there that can walk us through the steps, provide templates for formatting, and print our books on demand. This means you can order one copy or fifty and pay the same price per book, instead of having to order stacks of books that might gather dust in your garage for twenty years.

So grab a beverage of your choice, stick your Kindle or phone or book in a plastic baggie, and plan to read this chapter in a bubble bath, because it gets a little frustrating... so you might as well be relaxed when you read it.

SHOULD I PUBLISH MY BOOK IN PAPERBACK?

Almost 100% of the time, you should release your book for both paperback and Amazon Kindle. (There is also the option of 'going wide' with other digital formats, we'll cover that in Chapter 5.) Here are the reasons we very much recommend creating paperbacks:

- **They're physical.** Paperbacks can be sold at local markets such as bookstores and event booths.
- **They can possibly sell better than digital books.** Specific genres (such as workbooks, coffee table books and children's books) will

almost always sell better in physical copies than ebooks.

- **Perfect for speakers.** Authors who speak publicly, like pastors, teachers, and motivational speakers can have great paperback sales at their events.
- **Signed paperbacks are great for promotional giveaways.** They can also be given as gifts for family, friends, and beta readers.
- **They can be donated** to libraries, hospitals, schools, etc.
- **Many readers and collectors prefer them.** Paperback books smell better than Kindles. It's true. Some people prefer the old-fashioned feel of paperback books in their hands and may not even own an e-reader (this is especially true for certain types of books, like educational, historical, or biographical).
- **Higher profit margin.** Paperback copies normally have a higher profit margin for indie publishers than ebook sales. For example, Jamie's novel *Sentinel* makes $1.88 profit for every Kindle copy sold, but $4.59 for every paperback sold through Amazon/CreateSpace. And she makes a whopping $10.59 for every paperback she sells herself through events.

HOW MUCH WILL MY PAPER-BACK COST TO PRODUCE?

This is one of the questions we are asked the most, and it's probably because people still think they'll have to pay a fortune to some vanity press to get their book produced. The awesome truth is that, if you *really* need to, you can produce a paperback for free, and only have to pay the printing cost for each physical copy.

Assuming you already have your manuscript and editing complete and a cover ready, there are possible 3 costs associated with the production of a paperback:

1. **Formatting: $0 - $500.** We highly recommend leaving this to the

professionals unless you're a professional graphic artist yourself and/or very tech savvy. It isn't for the faint of heart—formatting is normally the most excruciating part of the publishing process.

That being said, you can attempt to format your book yourself using a template for Microsoft Word. We've detailed this process in a section later in this chapter. Angela's an ace at this. Or if you're a professional designer familiar with Adobe InDesign, you can create your own high-resolution, print-ready PDF with only the cost of your own time.

But if you're looking to spare yourself a lot of migraines and leave the formatting to the pros, companies like Book Baby can take your Microsoft Word document and do all the formatting for you. A normal cost for a formatting package (including both paperback and Kindle) is generally around $300-$500. There's a calculator on their website at bookbaby.com.

2. **ISBN: $0 - $125.** You can get an ISBN for free through the print-on-demand printer, CreateSpace. Or if you want to keep all the rights to your ISBN, you can purchase one through Bowker at www.myidentifiers.com for $125. Or if you're planning on making a career out of indie publishing, you can buy 10 ISBNs in bulk for about $300.

You will need a different ISBN for paperback and hardcover editions of your book if you decide to have both available. However, ebooks do not require ISBNs. Yay!

Why would you want to keep the rights? If you decide to publish with a different printer or distributor besides CreateSpace, you will have to use an ISBN that you own.

Also, if you use a free ISBN from CreateSpace, they will be listed as the publisher on your book listing (including on your book's Amazon page). Many voracious readers are in-the-know enough to realize that this means you're indie published, so it might mean certain readers and bloggers could discriminate against you. And if you decide to publish your books under your own press name (more on that in Chapter 5), you won't be able to include that in your Amazon listing with a CreateSpace ISBN.

If you are just starting out and you're concerned about money, you can absolutely use CreateSpace's ISBN. You can always decide to buy your own later on down the road.

3. **Proofing: $0 - $10 per copy.** A proof copy from a print-on-demand printer generally costs less than $10 ($2.50 - $4.50 is our average, depending on the book's page count, dimensions, whether or not it has color in the interior, and other factors). You'll have to pay for shipping as well. A proof copy is optional, but we highly recommend you order a physical proof copy to look over and make sure it's formatted correctly before you hit the big red 'publish' button (especially if you have done the formatting yourself).

    Or if you're very experienced and/or confident, CreateSpace gives you the option to skip the paperback proof and look over your manuscript online with a digital proofing tool instead. This option is free.

Are you still following? Good. If you need to take a break and catch some episodes of *Doctor Who* or *Gilmore Girls* or whatever you binge-watch, we totally understand. We didn't write this chapter in one go, either. There was plenty of wine involved.

WHICH PRINTER SHOULD I CHOOSE?

CREATESPACE

CreateSpace is the print-on-demand service that we have both used to host our paperbacks across the board. With a few exceptions that have always been made right, CreateSpace delivers affordable, professional products in a relatively slow but reliable time. (Imagine us biting our fingernails, waiting at the door for the package, because we procrastinated and didn't order our books in time for a signing. It's happened far more often than we'd like to admit. And will probably happen again, to be truthful.)

Amazon owns CreateSpace, so they will automatically create an Amazon.com listing for your paperback and sell it through the Amazon website. When a paperback copy of your book is sold on Amazon, CreateSpace will print it, ship it, and pay you a commission. You don't have to do a thing. It's pretty awesome.

CreateSpace is free to use up front, and they charge a very reasonable price per printed book (the exact price depends on the length, size, and specifications of the book—bigger books will naturally cost more to produce). Shipping cost is based on number of books purchased. There is no fee for production or set-up. You can use their Royalty Calculator to determine the price for printing your book at https://www.createspace.com/Products/Book under the 'Royalties' tab.

If you don't live in the United States and wish to order paperbacks, be prepared to pay quite a bit more for shipping from CreateSpace. Currently they do not have international printing available.

If you need to make edits after you've published with CreateSpace, you can change everything except the book's title, cover, and author name for free. But the book's title, cover, and author name can never be changed. You will have to create a new book listing for that—with a new ISBN. But it's not as complicated as it sounds.

Another thing about CreateSpace to keep in mind: They do not produce hardcover books. So if you're looking for hardcover, a different printer like Book Baby or Lulu might be a good choice. Just expect to pay a much higher price per copy.

INGRAMSPARK

IngramSpark is another excellent print-on-demand printer, but they're best known for their huge range of distributors for ebooks and paperbacks alike. They also offer the option to create hardcover copies. Here are a few things to consider about IngramSpark (besides the name—isn't it cool? Almost seems like the name of a starship from some distant galaxy):

- IngramSpark allows you to choose if your books are returnable or not. Most bookstores will only purchase books if they are returnable, and CreateSpace does not allow returns.
- While CreateSpace allows you to use their service for free (aside from the possible ISBN cost), IngramSpark has a per-book fee based on which formats you want to print in. At the time of this release, the price for setting up a new print book is $49.
- IngramSpark, like many other printers, does not provide a free ISBN like CreateSpace does. So you will need to purchase an ISBN from Bowker to print with them.
- IngramSpark is a great choice if you are publishing a book for children. They offer a better distribution plan to libraries and bookstores that can also benefit authors outside of the United States.

- If you find a typo in your book after you've finalized everything with IngramSpark and have to upload a revised file, they charge you a fee of $25.

RETURNABILITY: GETTING YOUR INDIE BOOKS ON REAL BOOKSHELVES

There are tons of bookstores out there—especially the smaller businesses—who refuse to work with CreateSpace. Why? Because CreateSpace doesn't allow them to return books that won't sell.

IngramSpark gives you the ability to choose whether or not your book is returnable. Even though making your book returnable might mean you have to pay for an occasional return, we highly recommend allowing returns. It will get your books onto so many more shelves than before, creating opportunities for sales that wouldn't exist otherwise.

However, just because you publish with IngramSpark does not guarantee your book will automatically be in the front window of every Barnes & Noble. Your book will still have to be amazing to be selected by brick and mortar stores.

KDP'S NEW PAPERBACK SERVICE

In 2017, Amazon KDP (Kindle Direct Publishing) began to offer authors the opportunity to publish paperbacks with them directly instead of going through CreateSpace. There are pros and cons to this arrangement.

Note: Please check the website to verify this information, as these policies could have changed since we published this book. A lot of these changes are brand new as we write this!

PROS
- You can easily see paperback sales and Kindle sales in one place (the good 'ole KDP Dashboard) instead of switching back and forth to different websites.
- If you make changes to your paperback book on CreateSpace for any reason, readers will not be able to purchase the book until the changes are fixed, which can mess with your book's rankings and other algorithms. But with KDP, your book remains available even while changes are being made.
- Kindle Select paperbacks are slightly easier to upload and set up.

CONS
- As of this book's publishing (May 2018), Amazon KDP does not offer the expanded distribution channels CreateSpace gives.
- Once you've uploaded your book to KDP, they do not want you to use any other printing service. Just like KDP Select/Kindle Unlimited, Amazon is greedy with exclusivity.
- With CreateSpace, you will receive a payout thirty days after each month your books make money. With KDP, you will have to wait sixty days, just like you have to for your ebook royalties.

The steps you work through to format a print book will pretty much be the same as CreateSpace, but when you upload the manuscript, the directions you will follow will be similar to uploading an Amazon Kindle book. Check Chapter 5: Ebook Formatting and the Kindle Monster for tips on formatting ebooks.

PICTURES AND COLOR AND POP-UPS, OH MY

DIMENSIONS

We recommend you go to the library or bookstore and check out a few other books in your genre. Check out how the covers look with different lengths, widths, margins, font sizes, and the spacing between lines of text.

The best size for your book will vary with its genre and length. We both prefer the standard size—6 inches x 9 inches—for the most part, but it's completely up to you.

> If your book has detailed illustrations in its interior, you might want choose a larger page size so the detail will be easier to make out once it's printed.

A book with more pages will generally cost more to produce, especially from a print-on-demand printer like most indies use. So consider using a larger size like 6"x9" and make sure that your formatter knows to focus on reducing page count.

COLOR IS EXTRA

If you are planning a picture book or another type of book with full-color art, keep in mind that the print copies you purchase from your printer will cost more. CreateSpace has a handy-dandy calculator where you can plug in your book's trim size, length, and color preference, so you can get an idea before you start of how much those dazzling colors will cost you. Check it out at https://www.createspace.com/Products/Book under the 'Royalties' tab.

Even one interior color page will cost the same as the entire book being full color, so keep that in mind. Maybe your imaginary country of Blinn's map would be better on the back cover, where it can reside in full-color splendor without costing you (and your readers) extra. It's up to you.

PICTURES AND ILLUSTRATIONS

If you want to add special formatting such as illustrations, photos, and bracketed sections, it *can* be done with the free Microsoft Word templates for CreateSpace, but, well… it can be extremely frustrating. Special formatting is much easier with more advanced formatting programs like InDesign, so if you aren't familiar with that, we recommend paying a professional formatter (at least for your first effort).

We hate having to point you elsewhere, but there are so many variations/complications that we recommend searching for tutorial videos on YouTube for your specific needs if you're going to attempt special formatting in a Microsoft Word template for CreateSpace.

POP-UP, LIFT-THE-FLAP, AND SPECIALTY BOOKS

This type of book can be extremely expensive to produce, and from what we have learned, most of the companies that produce them for indie publishers are all out of the United States. This is not to say it can't be done; it will just take time and effort on your part to figure it out.

Do keep in mind that any child's book is a risk when self-publishing (kind of like giving one of these books to a two-year-old), and if you throw a ton of money into a pop-up book you might never get it back. Your best bet might be to try to pitch your specialty book to a traditional publisher that already specializes in that field.

A THIN SILVER LINING

When you have your work on the internet in any form, it will be pirated. Because people are evil and they like to steal things.

Both Jamie and Angela have their books floating around on all sorts of nefarious sites, and unfortunately it's the same situation for traditionally published authors. Does it keep them from selling books? No. Is there anything they can do about it? Other than reporting the site—sadly not.

But look on the bright side: many marketing strategies revolve around giving away the first book in a series for free anyway. If people find your first book for free on a pirate site, there's always a chance they could become a fan and buy your other books.

PIRATES AND BOOTY (YARRR!)

COPYRIGHT

One of the first things a new-to-publishing author worries about is the copyright issue—people stealing your work. And yes, it's a valid concern. Websites pirate books every day... it's a sad fact of life.

Once you have published a book under your name, it's legally your property and copyright, therefore, you can say 'copyright (your name)' on the back cover and front page of your book with all legality.

However, if someone decides to come up and contest your work, you might have to prove with original, dated files that is, in fact, your original writing. So keep everything. On the bright side, we've only heard of this happening to handful of writers in the last several years.

If you live in the United States, you can register your copyright with the government copyright services at https://eco.copyright.gov. It costs about $35 per book.

Will this keep your work from being pirated? Probably not. Do we think it's absolutely necessary? Nope. But if it makes you feel better, go right ahead.

PRICING

If you offer your books through the CreateSpace platform, you will be shown a calculator where you can input the price of your book to see what profit you will make when someone purchases it through Amazon.com, your CreateSpace page (which may be removed with the introduction of Amazon's new paperback service), or an expanded distribution website like your local bookstore or Barnes & Noble.

CreateSpace will have a minimum price you can charge, because they need to make a cut of the sale as well (after all, they are printing and shipping the book). For example, if the CreateSpace cut for your book is

$5.49 (it will be different for every book) and you decide to charge $10.99, you will receive $5.50 in profit.

Here are some things to consider when setting your paperback price:

- **Contrast and compare.** Market research is a good idea, we recommend you compare prices to other paperback books on Amazon of similar length. Consider pricing your book a few dollars lower than *new* (not used) copies of bestselling books in your genre.
- **Watch your expanded distribution profit.** Because CreateSpace and Amazon take out quite a large piece of the pie, you will generally only receive a few dollars from each book you sell. This can turn into only a few cents for books that sell from expanded distribution.
- **Keep the price low to encourage sales.** For most genres, paperbacks will only be a small percentage of your sales. And the higher your paperback price, the less sales it's likely to receive. We recommend you keep the price low, especially for children's books and the first book in a series.

CREATESPACE TUTORIALS

MICROSOFT WORD TEMPLATES FOR CRE-ATESPACE

Unless you happen to be some kind of graphic designer InDesign wonder woman like Jamie, or have the funds to pay a professional formatter, you will probably want to use a premade Microsoft Word template for your book and upload it to CreateSpace (or the printer of your choice).

A template will have the chapter headers, paragraphs, spacers, and other elements set in place, so all you have to do is replace with your own text. You can download a generic template from CreateSpace, or purchase fancier ones from companies like Creative Market at https://creativemarket.com/search?q=book+template.

You can find plenty of websites that offer a variety of formats for free, but always check carefully for viruses before you download.

A STEP-BY-STEP TUTORIAL FOR CRE-ATESPACE'S STANDARD TEMPLATE

Please note: These instructions are *very* basic. We can't get into technical matters like "Help, I can't figure out how to get the page header off of page 27!" CreateSpace offers multiple tutorial videos for formatting if you get stuck, and we recommend you refer to them if you get in a bind. For more information about front and back matter, please refer to Chapter 7: Bells and Whistles: Categories, Keywords, Blurbs, and More.

1. **Download the template** for the size of book you have chosen (dimensions such as 6"x9", 5"x7", etc) from this link: https://www.createspace.com/Products/Book/InteriorPDF.jsp

2. **Create the title page.** If you like, you can choose a fancy font for your title and chapter headers. CreateSpace might ding you for this later, saying they had to change the font around to embed it correctly and it might not look right, but as long as it looks good on the print preview you should be okay.

   If you'd like to find a free, fancy font you don't already have, check out fontsquirrel.com or fonts.google.com (Google Fonts can also be embedded on your website if you'd like it to match). Just make sure the font is legible and easy to read. For the rest of the text, Garamond, Minion Pro, or just plain Times New Roman can all be good choices.

3. **Fill in the ISBN.** If you haven't purchased an ISBN yet and you plan to get one free with CreateSpace, you can wait on this step, but don't forget before you finish it up.

4. **Write your acknowledgments** if you have any.

5. **Don't forget to dedicate** your book to someone special!

6. **Make space for any special sections.** CreateSpace's template doesn't have a space for an author's note, so you'll have to create a section for one, as well as any prologues, glossaries, pronunciation guides, casts of characters, or any other front matter. Make sure you insert a section break after each one of these.

7. **Table of Contents.** You aren't required to have this for a paperback book, but if you want one, put a place marker for it and save this step for last. You won't know which page each chapter begins on until your formatting is finished. Don't forget to come back and fill in the page numbers!

8. **Design the look of the chapter headers.** In front of each chapter, you should place the chapter number using the awesome font you chose. We recommend you look at other books in your genre to get an idea of spacing and font size. You should begin the chapter header about two-thirds down the page.

   And if you like, you can also add a little more pizazz with chapter titles, quotes in front of each chapter, or drop caps (where the first letter of each chapter's text appears larger).

9. **Duplicate for each chapter.** Once you have a nice style for the front of each chapter, you can copy and paste the formatting for each chapter as many times as needed.

   If you have a lot of chapters, it's a good idea to copy multiple instances of your chapter numbers to save time. For example, if you have 40 chapters, you can copy 10 instances of your chapter formatting and paste it 4 times to quickly create entries for 40 chapters.

10. **Input your writing.** Copy and paste the text of your chapters into the template beneath each chapter's heading. Your text should be justified, your paragraphs shouldn't have a space between them, and your first lines should be indented by 0.5" (about five spaces). Your lines should be spaced at 1.5 lines apart. Repeat with each chapter.

11. **Eradicate pesky symbols.** After you have all of your text inserted, check over the entire book with the 'show symbols' option on. This will help you catch any weird spacing or formatting issues, including page breaks and section breaks.

12. **Design the header & footer.** Fill in your author name and the book title in header. Put automatic page numbers in the footer.

13. **Create the back matter.** Add your author biography and back matter (more on this in Chapter 7). Don't forget to include a link where people can sign up for your email newsletter, your website info, and other social media links. And make sure you nicely request an honest review.

Don't use Apple Pages for formatting your book. For some mysterious reason unbeknownst to us, CreateSpace and Pages do not get along, and as far as we know, will not work together as friends.

PUBLISHING YOUR PAPERBACK ON CRE-ATESPACE

Here's a quick list of what you will need to list your book on CreateSpace, from information to files:

- **Title information.** Remember, once your book is published *this can't be changed,* so make sure there are no errors. Enter your book's title, series information, your author name, and any contributors such as illustrators.

- **ISBN.** Once your ISBN is locked in, *it cannot be changed* without creating a new book inside CreateSpace. Don't forget to add it to your book's interior (normally it's with copyright information on the bottom of one of the very first pages).

- **Formatted interior file.** Make sure your book's interior file is PDF, DOC, DOCX, or RTF format, and that your book is formatted *exactly* the way you want it. Any images inside should be high-resolution (300 DPI). You will have a chance to preview your interior in the aptly named interior reviewer tool.

- **Cover spread file.** You will have three options for uploading your cover. You can use the CreateSpace cover creator and add your own photos and font, you can pay someone from CreateSpace to design a cover for you, or you can upload a complete PDF design.

Assuming you hired a professional cover designer, they should deliver the final artwork in the form of a PDF called a cover spread. It spread should include the front cover, spine, and back cover. Check out Chapter 3: How to Make a Bad Book Cover, Guaranteed for more technical details.

Once you've uploaded your cover spread (it usually takes a

few minutes since high-resolution files tend to be large), choose whether you'd like your cover to be matte or glossy. This is more personal preference than anything.

- **Time: the file review process.** CreateSpace will review your files and let you know if there are any issues. This usually takes about 24 hours. You will then be required to proof your book online, or order a physical proof. We highly, *highly* recommend you order a physical proof to check your cover and formatting. But know that ordering a physical proof will require you to wait for the proof's shipping time, whereas a digital proof will allow you to put your book up for sale immediately.

- **Channels.** You will be able to choose what channels you wish for your book to be available on. These are the places your paperback book will be available to order, such as Amazon. com, libraries, and bookstores. If you're creating a memoir or personal family book, then you won't want to offer your book for distribution at all. But if you're wanting to sell your book, you will want to choose all the available options.

  Just keep in mind if you choose expanded distribution, you won't get the same amount per sale as you would if you sell through Amazon. And you will not have control over these sales in any way, shape, or form. But on the bright side, you will have your books available for a larger audience.

- **Price.** This will allow you to input a price and see how much royalty you will get from each channel for what you charge. This also shows you the payouts from other countries. Yes, you can charge $100 per book... but you probably won't make any sales.

- **Description.** This will be the description and category customers see on all of your book's sales pages like Amazon and Barnes & Noble's websites. It's best to keep this simple, without any HTML or special characters, because they may not display properly across all websites. For more ideas about writing description, go to Chapter 7: Bells and Whistles: Categories, Keywords, Blurbs, and More.

- **Publish on Kindle.** You will be directed to the Kindle Direct Publishing website from here to publish your Kindle book. We cover this in Chapter 5.

ARE YOU STILL THERE?

Whew. That was intense. Let's just take a deep breath.

Complicated is an understatement, huh? Yeah. This is why we recommend that non-techies pay for formatting—especially beginners. A few hundred bucks can seem like a steep price, but if it spares you days of headaches, it might just be worth saving up for.

Don't lose heart! This is the most complicated part of the whole publishing process. It gets easier with time—and there are more fun ventures ahead!

QUESTIONS

1. Should I try to format my book on my own or pay for a professional service? What are the pros and cons for my project?
2. Should I pay for a fancy template and risk complications, or keep it plain with CreateSpace's official template?
3. Which formats do I want to publish for (paperback, Kindle, other ebook readers, hardcover, audio, etc.)? Which ones are worth the up-front formatting cost, and which ones are most likely to pay off in the long run?

Chapter 5

EBOOK FORMATTING
AND THE KINDLE MONSTER

> *"Lovers of print are simply confusing the plate for the food."*
>
> — Douglas Adams

Ebook formatting has its quirks, but it's not as tedious as paperback formatting (at least in our opinion). The hardest part is over. Take a deep breath. Pat yourself on the back. You've got this!

If you don't read on Kindle or another e-reader, this might be completely alien territory. But when it comes to sales for most indie writers, Kindle is king. Neither one of us would have had nearly the sales we've had today if it weren't for the Kindle and ebook platform. Fortunately, formatting your book for Kindle doesn't have to be that bad—in fact, potty training was much more intimidating. And messy.

There are all kinds of ebook readers out there, but only two major ebook formats: MOBI and EPUB. Kindle's exclusive format is MOBI, but EPUB works for any ebook reader *except* for Kindle.

We recommend that every author publish for Kindle because, well, it's free to upload a book to KDP (Kindle Direct Publishing) and list it for sale on Amazon.com. And here are a few other reasons:

- **Free for readers even if they don't have a Kindle.** Kindle is a platform anyone with a smartphone or PC can access *for free*. Just download the free Kindle app and you won't have to purchase a Kindle device in order to read Kindle books. Sweet!
- **The world's bestselling bookstore.** 55% of all books sold in 2017 were ebooks,* and 82% of ebook sales were on the Kindle platform.* Kindle's market share grows even higher for adult fiction, especially romance, where 90% of books sold are ebooks.

2017 BOOK SALES

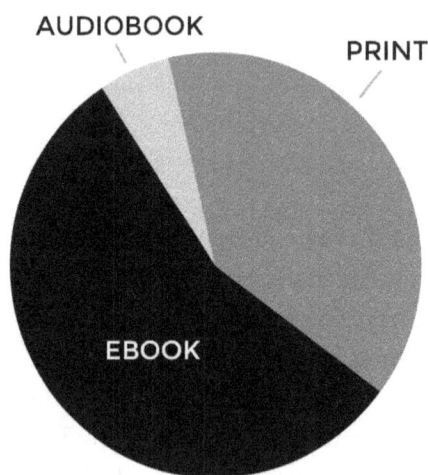

AUDIOBOOK

PRINT

EBOOK

EBOOK SALES

B&N NOOK

APPLE IBOOKS   OTHER

AMAZON

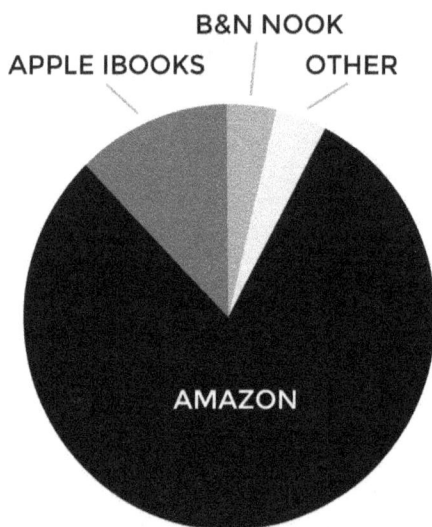

Statistics taken from AuthorEarnings.com

- **Many people prefer their e-reader.** Kindle books can be preferred over physical copies for many reasons: cost, accessibility, shelf space, the ability to adjust the font size and background color, and the ability to have a whole library in the palm of your hand.

- **An international marketplace.** Your books will reach a worldwide market (Amazon.com), whose audience might not be willing to pay the cost of international shipping for your paperback.
- **Excellent marketing opportunities.** Having a Kindle book allows you to use AMS—Amazon Marketing Services, which has proven to be a great return on investment for our books.
- **Send free copies** to proofers, beta teams, reviewers, and bloggers instead of having to pay to print and ship them.
- **Awesome for indies.** If you're an indie, Kindle sales will be your bread and butter—a steady stream of income. This is where the majority of Angela's and Jamie's income is from.

FORMATTING YOUR BOOK FOR KINDLE

If you don't have the funds to pay a professional to format your Kindle book, you can do it yourself, but just like paperbacks, a distinct learning curve is involved.

There are two main ways to creating your own Kindle ebook: with a Microsoft Word template or with HTML (if you happen to be a code wizard).

SHORTCUT! USING A PAPERBACK TEMPLATE

Most of the time, if you have already formatted a book for CreateSpace with a Microsoft Word template, you can create a hyperlinked table of contents (here's a video tutorial: https://youtu.be/KL3FIBZAeJI), remove the headers and footers, and upload away. KDP will create a Kindle book based on your Word document.

If you use your paperback file, you will not keep any fancy fonts you've inserted (Kindle allows users to set their own fonts, so most custom fonts are stripped from Kindle files). Images, however, should stay the way they are.

If fancy is important to your book, you will have to format your book in HTML or hire someone to do it for you.

IF YOU DON'T HAVE A PAPERBACK EDITION, AND AREN'T PLANNING ON CREATING ONE...

You can still use a CreateSpace template for free, or download a free Kindle template online (there are lots to choose from).

OM NOM NOM

Although uploading a Word template for your Kindle book can work fabulously, it's just a computer crunching up your Word document and spitting it back out in Kindle format. Which could look just fine, or like your aunt's attempt at meatloaf. It's also known to start whining the second it sees something it doesn't like.

Sometimes issues you can't see in your Word document are translated into monsters in the Kindle format. Angela had problems she couldn't find once, and Amazon flagged her book page for formatting errors. She ended up having to get the formatting re-done by a professional formatter.

To format a Kindle book, you will pretty much follow the directions from Chapter 4, except:

- You don't need headers and footers (just go the headers/footers section and remove them)
- You need a hyperlinked table of contents at the beginning of the book, per Amazon's rules (you run the risk of them removing your book otherwise).
- You need to make sure all included links are highlighted as links so when people touch them on their screen, their Kindle/phone will take them to that website.

TIPS AND TAGS FOR THE CODE MONKEYS

This section is for those familiar with HTML and CSS. If looking at code raises your blood pressure, please, by all means, skip this section as fast as you can.

HTML tags allowed in Kindle books are *very* basic. Forget most of the fancy tricks you know and check out the supported tags here: https://kdp.amazon.com/en_US/help/topic/G200673180

There are also three custom tags just for Kindle ebooks:

- **<mbp:pagebreak>** - Forces a page break.
- **<mbp:nu>** - Formats enclosed text as "not underlined." (Overrides <font> tag attributes.)
- **<mbp:section>** - Defines a book section.

CSS can be used, but it must be contained in a dedicated CSS file, which is separate from your HTML content. Use a link tag to point your HTML to your CSS file. In the same way, your images will be separate files that will be uploaded together in a ZIP file with the rest of your collection.

But the options with CSS are also very limited. Because Kindle devices (and the Kindle app) allow the user to choose their own font face, font size, and colors (as well as background color), the Kindle website will strip any unsupported code upon upload.

Because Jamie doesn't want to memorize every tag that's allowed or not, she uses the Kindle Previewer program to test out how things are looking as she goes. It lets you see how your Kindle book will look on several different devices with varying screen sizes. You can download it for free here: https://www.amazon.com/gp/feature. html?ie=UTF8&docId=1000765261

And here is the link to Kindle's HTML Formatting Guidelines: https://kdp.amazon.com/en_US/help/topic/G200673220 Good luck, and have fun!

HOW TO UPLOAD YOUR BOOK TO KINDLE DIRECT PUBLISHING

1. **Create an account.** If you don't already have an account, create one at kdp.amazon.com. Make sure you have a bank account connected for receiving royalty payments. You also need to submit your tax information.

2. **Submit a new title for your book.** Find "Create a New Title" and click "Kindle eBook."

3. **Fill in the details.** Make sure you fill out the title and your author's name exactly the way it is on the cover. Here you can also dictate the series information, the description as it will appear on your book page, keywords, categories, and more. (For more information on book details, go to Chapter 7.)

4. **Select a release date.** Choose if you would like to release book now, or put it up for pre-order. You can set up a pre-order up to 90 days in advance. (More information about pre-orders in Chapter 8: Pre-Marketing: Preparing for Launch.)

5. **Fill out the content page.** Upload your manuscript in its Microsoft Word template or HTML/CSS glory (or if your formatter gave you another format like MOBI, that will work too). Once you have uploaded the book's interior, you will be able to preview what your book will look like on an e-reader with the Online Previewer tool. To access this, wait until the upload completes, then hit the "Launch Previewer" button at the bottom of the page. Next, upload your cover image and make sure to hit "Save."

6. **Determine your price.** Choose if you want to enroll in the KDP Select program and what price you want to charge. We have dedicated sections to help you make both of these decisions below.

7. **Give your readers some cool perks.** Decide if you want your book to be offered as part of the Lending Library, which means customers can loan the book to family and friends for up to 14 days.

   Then consider joining the Kindle Matchbook program, which allows customers who have purchased the paperback version of a book to get a discount on their Kindle version. Whether or not you check these is completely up to you, but remember as an indie author, the more books out there the better.

PRICING STRATEGIES

KDP allows you to choose between two royalty options: 35% and 70%. To qualify for the 70% rate, your book must be priced between $2.99 and $9.99. Books in the 70% range also must pay a Delivery Fee based on your book's file size. Check out the section below for more information on this fee.

Deciding on a price for your ebook is a bit different than paperback pricing. Like paperbacks, we suggest you check other *indie* kindle book prices in similar genres. A traditionally published author with a huge audience is going to be able to charge a lot more for a Kindle book than an unknown indie author. It's just the way it is. (Of course, when you're super famous and have a million fans, you can up the price with the click of a mouse.)

Different indie authors will tell you different strategies, but we suggest you start with your prices as follows and see how they go.

- **Short stories:** $0.99
- **Short how-to books or devotionals under 200 pages:** $2.99
- **Children's books and books under 200 pages:** $2.99
- **Novels or non-fiction with 200-300 pages:** $3.99-$4.99
- **Novels over 300 pages:** Use discretion, but Jamie doesn't recommend that indies price any single novel higher than $5.99. Her whopping 390-page book *Sage* is priced at $4.99 and does very well.
- **Boxed sets:** The cost of the individual books minus a few dollars. We recommend not going higher than $9.99 so you can stay within Kindle's 70% royalty range.

If you are publishing a series, consider pricing the first book at a dollar or two less than the other books in a series. Better to rake in more sales and get a little less money, but get more readers hooked.

AMAZON'S SNEAKY FEE: THE DOWNLOAD DOWNLOW

Amazon charges a Delivery Fee for every Kindle ebook sale at the 70% royalty rate, and they're not super up-front about it. They charge $0.15 per MB (megabyte), which might not seem like much, but like extra pictures from your kid's school photo day, it can add up *quick*. Especially if you have a lot of images inside your book that increases its file size.

For example, if your book is 4 megabytes, you will pay an additional $0.60 cents along with Amazon's cut from your royalties for *every sale*.

KDP Pricing Support (Beta)
See the relationship between price and past sales and author earnings for KDP books like yours.

View Service

Select a royalty plan and set your Kindle eBook list prices below

○ 35%

◉ 70%

i Your book file size after conversion is 2.09 MB.

Primary Marketplace	List Price		Rate	Delivery	Royalty
Amazon.com ⇕	$ 2.99	USD	35% ▾	$0.00	$1.05
	Must be $2.99-$9.99 ▾ All marketplaces are based on this price		70%	$0.31	$1.88

Other Marketplaces (12) ⌄

Novels and chapter books with one or two graphics won't usually be charged very much, but authors of graphic novels and children's books with lots of illustrations should beware. Jamie found that she was being charged an arm and a leg for her *Sentinel Trilogy* box set with all of its map graphics and fancy appendix images. We also had trouble reducing the file size of our *Busy Mom* books with all of the art assets.

You can check your converted book size on the Amazon pricing page to see what your book's delivery fee will be. For Amazon's fine print on delivery fees, check out this page: https://kdp.amazon.com/en_US/help/topic/G200634500

SHOULD I ENTER THE KDP SELECT PROGRAM OR 'GO WIDE?'

Amazon's KDP Select program allows books to be featured in the Kindle Unlimited program. This is like Netflix for books—readers pay one flat subscription fee and get access to any Kindle Unlimited book they want with no added cost. This is where the most voracious 'serial readers' tend to snatch their books from, because it ends up being cheaper for them in the long run.

Authors in the KDP Select program are paid via KENP (Kindle Edition Normalized Pages) Read. Amazon calculates how many pages its users read of your Kindle books, adds them up, and pays authors a fraction of a cent per page read. This amount varies depending on the month—it's calculated by how many pages were read by Kindle Unlimited subscribers overall that month and divided equally—but Jamie uses the average calculation of $0.0045 times her Pages Read count to estimate her royalties.

This may not sound like a lot, but boy, it adds up.

Below is Jamie's sales report for October 2017. On one day she had only 3 pages read, but on others, thanks to a free pulsing promotion (check out our free pulsing strategy in *The Busy Mom's Guide to Novel Marketing)*, on some days she had over 4,000 pages read. The total for the month added up to 54,148 pages read.

By Jamie's estimate, this means a total of $243.66 in royalties for her that month from Kindle Unlimited alone. Her Kindle book sales that month were only slightly higher, meaning she almost doubled her income by being enrolled in KDP Select and using its promotion options (namely, the 5 free days that each book can use per 90-day period).

The 5 free days allowed to KDP Select books are the foundation of Angela and Jamie's free pulsing marketing strategy that works so well for them (illustrated in the graphic below). That alone is a big reason to consider enrolling your book in KDP Select.

Units Ordered (What's this?) ▾

Paid Units Ordered (eBook) ✔   Paid Units Shipp

Kindle Edition Normalized Pages (KENP) Read from KU and KOLL (What's this?) ▾

Kindle Edition Normalized Pages (KENP) Read from KU and KOLL ✔

SO WHAT'S THE CATCH?

Well… it's a pretty big catch. To enroll in KDP Select, Amazon requires authors to remain exclusive to them, meaning they can't put their enrolled book up on any other ebook platform—including Barnes & Noble Nook, Kobo, and even PDF copies on your own website—for the 90-day enrollment period.

Ouch.

But unfortunately, the competition just can't keep up with Amazon at the moment. The amount of books sold on Barnes & Noble Nook and other platforms are negligible compared to Kindle for most authors. (As always, there are author and genre exceptions.) Nook in particular has lost more than half its value in just over two years.*

However, the idea of 'going wide'—formatting your book for all platforms (including Kindle, just not enrolling in the exclusive KDP Select program)—can have its own benefits. Naturally there are some readers who who don't prefer Kindle who will be missing out on your books unless you go wide, and some genres of books do better on multiple

Author Lingo: 'GO WIDE'

If an author has 'gone wide', it means they have published their books for many ebook platforms (Kindle but also Nook, Kobo, iBooks, etc.) and therefore has chosen not to enroll in the exclusive KDP Select/Kindle Unlimited program.

PROS OF GOING WIDE

- Books are available for more kinds of e-readers, which means they will have more range and visibility.
- The first book in a series can be made permanently free (aka 'permafree'). If you have a large series, this can be a great way to snag readers on a continual basis.
- You will not be subjected to the Amazon monopoly; if you are only using Amazon as a distributor, it means they pretty much have complete control of your title.
- You can offer your book for free for promotions with no restrictions or worries. If you are with KDP Select, you're not allowed to offer your book for free on any other site or publish more than 10% of your book to read for previews, even on your own website.
- You can always try out the KDP Select program for a few months and see if it works for you. If you enroll in KDP Select, you will be locked in for 90 days.

CONS OF GOING WIDE

- Not being in Kindle Unlimited means you're missing out on potential royalties from Pages Read—Amazon tracks the number of pages people read and pays authors accordingly. This accounts for roughly half of Jamie and Angela's book-related income.
- Formatting for universal e-reader distribution can be difficult and time-consuming.
- You will not be allowed to take advantage of the Kindle Unlimited program, so you will not be able to utilize the exclusive promotions: either free days (5 per 90-day period) or Kindle Countdown deals. Not being able to run free promotions means you can't use our favorite marketing strategy, freepulsing (check out *The Busy Mom's Guide to Novel Marketing* for details).

platforms. It's also less scary for an author not to have all the eggs in the same basket, even if that basket is where the majority of income is.

Angela and Jamie are both currently KDP Select authors, because that's what works best for us right now. For more specific marketing strategies on how we make KDP Select work for us, check out the next book in this series, *The Busy Mom's Guide to Novel Marketing*.

FORMATTING FOR ALL OTHER EBOOKS: THE UNIVERSAL EPUB

There are so many different ways to format your book for the universal ebook format: EPUB, especially when you already have your book formatted for the Kindle MOBI format. Here are a few options:

- **Use a file converter.** There are lots of free tools online that can convert your MOBI file to an EPUB. Search for one and try it out, but beware of viruses and make sure to test your converted EPUB for issues before publishing it.
- **Try a free online creator.** Barnes & Noble offers a way to create your ebook on their website, and so do many other platforms that host and sell ebooks. Jamie has tried the Nook one and found it a bit finicky and glitchy, but hey, it's free and user-friendly. You should be able to download your EPUB file afterward.
- **Professional formatting.** If you've paid a pro to format your book for paperback and/or Kindle, the EPUB format is normally included. Formatting bundles like the ones offered at bookbaby. com can have great value and save you lots of time and stress in the long run.

QUESTIONS

1. What are the pros and cons of me hiring a pro to format my ebooks or trying to tackle it myself?
2. Does KDP Select sound right for me, or should I go wide?
3. What are similar books in my genre, of similar length, selling for in their ebook formats?

Chapter 6

AUDIOBOOKS

"Let go of expectations to a certain extent... Find a balance between achieving your vision and having some flexibility for small things that aren't that important."

— J. Grace Pennington, narrator of multiple audiobooks, including Angela's *Texas Women of Spirit* series

According to *The Good E-Reader,* the highest growing segment of publishing is audiobooks.* With the rise in use of phones for... well... everything, people are downloading audiobooks at an astonishing rate. Many people prefer audiobooks because they can listen to them in the car, while working out, doing laundry or dishes, or even when chasing wild children around their home.

Some indie authors don't even consider creating audiobooks because they don't own recording equipment and would have no idea how to produce such things. Professional narration seems like a pricey service to pay for. But these obstacles can be overcome.

RECORDING YOUR OWN AUDIOBOOKS

If you have any experience with recording or sound, you might want to set up your own recording studio. All you really need is a decent microphone—Jamie prefers the Blue Yeti, which is for sale on Amazon for around $100—and recording software. You don't need a fancy program—you can download Audacity for free after a quick internet search. Since you will probably use the equipment for more than one book, it could be a worthy investment (and a tax write-off).

> Jamie's favorite place to record is her closet, with her laptop and microphone on the dresser between the tunics and scarves. The hanging clothes **dampen unwanted noise,** and the door serves as a barrier between her and the crazy outside world.

But while it might be doable to type snatches of words here and there when kids are watching TV or playing quiet games (if there are any such things), finding uninterrupted quiet time for recording is probably more difficult. We don't know about you, but our children seem to lose their minds at the exact moment the phone rings! Some moms have created little sound studios in closets or outside sheds, or sacrificed some time during the night to record. And some find an accommodating friend or family member to loan them a space in a quieter home. Ah, doesn't that sound lovely?

Another issue you might have is your own narrative voice. You might be looking for a specific accent that you can't quite replicate. Or perhaps you'd prefer a narrator of the opposite gender. And let's face it: some people have better reading voices than others. If your children fall asleep halfway through the first *Little Critter* book, it might be a good idea to find a different narrator.

ACX TO THE RESCUE

If you choose to find a narrator for your audiobook, we have good news! There are hundreds of skilled, professional narrators just waiting to produce your book. One place to find them is on Audible's ACX—the Audiobook Creation Exchange.

Audible is Amazon's audiobook platform. They have several options when it comes to producing audiobooks. You can upload your own recording or you can hold auditions for narrators. When you post your book's audition, you can specify desired gender, age, and other particulars you are looking for in a narrator. And you can create a script with a sample of your writing (2-3 pages) for them to read from, then choose your favorite voice actor from the applicants.

Then when your book is produced, ACX will put your shiny new audiobook up for sale on your book's Amazon.com page as an available format beside your paperback and/or Kindle versions. Voila!

ROYALTY SHARE VS PAYMENT PER FINISHED HOUR

A great option Audible offers is the royalty share program. If you find a narrator who wants to work with you on your book, you can offer to share the royalties, which is 40 percent of sales, with the narrator, for seven years (which means both of you will receive 20 percent each). You don't pay a penny out of pocket.

On the other hand, if you'd rather make an up-front investment, you can opt to pay the narrator per recorded hour. This can end up being a rather hefty sum (normally a thousand dollars or more depending on the length of your book), but if you want to keep all profits, this is the way to go.

Keep in mind: If you opt for the royalty share program, there's a higher chance you will have less experienced narrators audition. This doesn't mean you can't find a great narrator, we just suggest you take care in whom you choose.

HOW MUCH MONEY WILL I MAKE ON AUDIOBOOK SALES?

The idea of having a professional narrate your creation can be pretty exciting. But we recommend holding off producing an audiobook for at least a few months before taking the plunge. See how your book does over a few months, and see how sales and ratings go. It can depend on genre, but a safe estimate of audio sales to Kindle sales ratio is about 1:10 to 1:20. (Sales numbers do not include free downloads if you do a free promotion with KDP Select). Some genres, like self-help, history, thrillers, and fantasy and sci-fi tend to perform better on audiobooks than business or children's books do.*

Audible's payout system can be difficult understand. At first, it *seems* like a lot, since your audiobook will be selling initially for around $15, where even 20% isn't a bad payout. And you might even receive $20 'bounties' which happen every time a customer chooses your book at the start of an Audible subscription. Sweet!

But Audible is notorious for changing costs around, running sales, and otherwise lowering prices. You will find you might earn several dollars on one sale, and only a few cents on another. And they will not contact you when they make these changes, so there's no warning or ability to opt in or out of a promotion.

Even considering this, Audible is the largest provider of digital audiobooks in the world, so most authors take the good with the irritating and move on.

CHOOSING A NARRATOR

Whether you choose to pay straight from your pocket or opt for the royalty share program, your voice actor can make or break audio sales (and the sales of the next book in your series). When you set up an audition on ACX.com, you will be posting a script—a short segment of your book that the prospective narrator will record and post for your approval. The book segment you choose is very important. We suggest choosing a section with some action/excitement, a section with a heartfelt moment, and at least two different characters 'speaking.'

When giving your audition guidance, be clear with your expectations. Make sure your prospective narrator knows the age, personality, and nationality of your main character. Be clear about the overall tone the narration should convey. If you want music at the beginning and end of the chapters/book, let them know.

Listen to the audition carefully. Make sure you consider several different narrators before you choose one, and if possible, listen to the sample book narrations on their page before you accept their offer.

Don't compromise, and don't be dazzled by an impressive resume. Even if a narrator has been in the business for years, that doesn't mean they are the best person to read your book. Just like everything else regarding your writing, you want the very best quality possible. Your book is worth it.

On the other hand, treat all auditions with respect. After all, they took the time to record a piece of your story. Be sure to thank each person who auditions.

Once you have made a decision, make sure you and your producer agree on a time of delivery. It may take a month or more for the book to be produced, depending on the length. Narrators often do ACX as a side job; they might even be writers with deadlines of their own.

Be respectful of the narrator's time. One hour of completed narration can take four or more hours to produce. Only ask for changes if they are absolutely necessary.

When the book is finished, be sure to listen to the entire narration from beginning to end. You can download it to your PC or your phone—Angela listened to hers while she folded laundry and drove the car. Make notes of any mistakes by chapter and page, so the narrator will be able to find the error and fix it quickly.

Listen for:

- **Exterior sounds,** such as slamming doors, dogs barking, etc.
- **Pacing problems.** Sections that are read too quickly, where the words are jumbled together. Pauses that are too long or occur in the middle of sentences.
- **Voice distinguishing.** In adult fiction, it's frowned upon for the narrator to talk exactly like the characters, however, it's important that listeners can distinguish a character is talking. The vocal inflection should be changed, but just slightly, not with great exaggeration. For children's books, however, more exaggeration can be used.
- **Proper nouns and other words that are mispronounced.** This especially pertains to historical and regional fiction, and sci-fi and fantasy worlds. Be sure to go over pronunciation with the narrator if you have unusual words or names.

> ## "Don't compromise... Just like everything else regarding your writing, you want the very best quality possible. Your book is worth it."

SELECTING MUSIC

You might have heard audiobooks that have music as 'bumpers' before and after the beginning of sections or chapters. This can be a nice, professional-sounding addition to your audiobook.

However, you need to make sure you are using music you have the rights to use. There are many sites that offer 'royalty-free' music of all different styles and emotions. You pay a one-time fee to have the rights to use this music for your product, similar to stock photos. One service that offers music like this is the Storyblocks site, audioblocks.com. This is also a handy site if you're looking for music for your website or YouTube book trailers.

AUDIOBOOK COVERS

Audible covers are required to be square, to have the book's title worded exactly the way it is on the Amazon listing, and to have the author's name. Sometimes you can rework the original book's cover like this (Angela reworked this one herself, but she's sure her cover designer Elaina Lee could have done a better job. She's just cheap.):

PRINT & EBOOK COVER

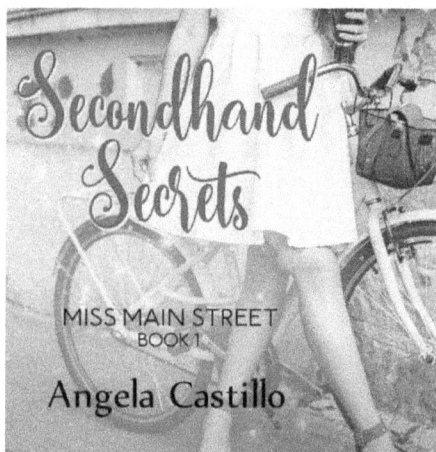

AUDIOBOOK COVER

ACX COUPONS

When your audiobook is approved, you can contact ACX at support@ acx.com for coupon codes for you to give out so people can download your audiobook for free. These make great prizes for newsletter giveaways, Facebook promotions, and blog post prizes. We recommend you give out as many as possible. Any reviews you can generate on Audible.com are awesome—they'll help you snatch more sales for your audiobooks in the future!

QUESTIONS

1. Do I want to produce an audiobook in the future? When? Should it release at the same time my paperback and/or Kindle release, or a few months later?

2. What kind of voice would best represent the characters and overall style of my book?

3. Would it be better long-term to save up to pay an experienced narrator up front, or should I consider a seven-year royalty share?

Chapter 7

BELLS AND WHISTLES:
CATEGORIES, KEYWORDS, BLURBS, AND MORE

"*The details are not the details. They make the design.*"

— Charles Eames

Even though Angela has written and published several paperback and Kindle books now, she always forgets about these little extra parts that end up being rather important. Kind of like when she goes into the laundry room and realizes the reason her kids have worn the same clothes for three days is because she hasn't done the wash for a week. In this chapter, we'll list the most common interior 'extras' so that hopefully, you can be more mindful of them and can set aside time to work on them.

Remember, any sections you include at the beginning will have to be flipped through before readers can get to the sample pages of the story for Amazon's 'look inside' preview of your Kindle book, so we recommend you limit the front extras to a few pages. Save lengthy glossaries and historic notes (especially of its for a fictional world) for the back of the book. Even J.R.R. Tolkien put his appendices in the back of his books way before Kindle was a thing.

FRONT MATTER: DOWN IN FRONT!

Dedication. This can be one line or a paragraph—we don't recommend making it longer than a few sentences. It's simply who you wrote the book for. We guarantee that even if your family doesn't read your book, they *will* flip to this page to see if they're on it.

We don't recommend you try to dedicate it to every friend or family member by name. Someone's going to be left out and have their feelings hurt. If you want to go this route we suggest a simple 'To all my family and friends.' Saves time and trouble.

Author's note (also known as a foreword). This is a good place to share a historical note, why the subject matter is meaningful to you, or anything else significant. Again, brevity is best.

Acknowledgments or thanks. This is different than a dedication, but can be combined with or used in place of a dedication. It could also go in the back of the book. You can thank whomever you wish, just try to keep it brief and no longer than one page. This is a great place to thank people who gave you information for your research, people who have inspired you in life, your editors, your babysitters...

Table of contents (TOC). Amazon Kindle books require a linked TOC—meaning the reader can click on an item in the table of contents and be taken to that section wherever it appears inside the book. These have proven to be a pain in the neck to Angela, who somehow forgets how to do this every time she formats a book and has to go back and find a tutorial like this one for Microsoft Word templates: https://youtu.be/

KL3FIBZAeJI She also has this trouble with long division; it might be a piece of cake to everyone else.

Cast of characters. If you have a large crew of people running rampant through your book, you might feel it's important to create a list to help your readers keep everyone straight. This is not always needed or recommended, but if you feel it's vital, again, keep it brief (one line of description per character, not a page).

Truthfully, if you feel this is required, your story might need some work to make it easier to digest. Your readers should get to know your characters slowly, through your story. But if you still feel this section is vital, we recommend you put it in the front, after all the other front matter but before the first chapter, so readers will know where to refer if needed. Do your best to make the whole section no longer than one page.

Map or magic system graphic. Some authors like to include a map of the territory, real or imagined, or a layout of a castle, carnival, fairgrounds, grand manor, or other kind of inserted art. If you decide to include this, make sure it's carefully done and the graphic is professional, sharp, and the font is easy to read. Also keep in mind Amazon's delivery fee. If the graphic resolution is too low it might be blurry, jagged or pixelated, but if the resolution is too high it could cost you a pretty penny in delivery fees. If in doubt, consult a graphic designer.

Editorial reviews or endorsements. If you have author buddies or friends in high places with nice things to say about your book, you might include a page with a list of your harmonious praise. If you decide to do this, keep it to only one page, please. Even though the Big 5 publishers tend to do include plenty of endorsements, readers can find pages of accolades annoying to flip through, and it takes up valuable real estate in your book's free Kindle preview on Amazon.com.

Prologue. Most stories can do without a prologue, and we highly recommend you weave any history into your current narration. If you must have a prologue, make it snappy, interesting, and brief. We go into this more in *The Busy Mom's Guide to Writing,* Chapter 6, 'Pitfalls to Avoid While Writing.'

BACK MATTER: JUNK IN THE TRUNK

Epilogue. Sometimes your story might need a little bit extra of a wrap-up, or perhaps a teaser for the next book in the series.

Glossary. Mostly used for books written about another country (or world). Good way to explain unfamiliar terms. Also found in fantasy and sci-fi as a part of the world building. Make sure this is included in your table of contents so your reader will know they can flip to it during the read, if need be.

Bibliography. A list of books used for reference or recommended for further reading on the subject. Or you might also have a list of sources (like the one in the back of this book). Check out Chapter 4 to see how to insert footers to direct readers to your glossary and/or bibliography.

About the author. A few paragraphs about who you are and what you have written. It's best to keep this personable and short. You can also include a professional photo of yourself, and links to where people can join your email newsletter, blog, social media, etc.

Request for a review. You can politely ask the reader to leave an *honest* review for your book when they're finished. This is a good way to slowly build up reviews over time.

Invitation to join your email newsletter list. Offer something juicy like a free short story to encourage readers to check out your website and/ or join your email newsletter list.

Promotions for your other work. When applicable, include sample chapters and lists of other books you have written to entice the reader to find more of your work.

SHOULD I NAME MY CHAPTERS?

It's perfectly acceptable to simply number your chapters, as long as you have a table of contents at the front of the book with hyperlinks. Or you can use the numbers spelled out or Roman numerals.

Here are some ideas for naming chapters:

- Think of a teaser header that entices the reader to dig into the chapter right away, like 'The Secret at the Top of the Hill.'
- Name each chapter a line from a famous poem, or lines from different poems from one famous poet.
- Chose a quote or scripture verse and use a few words for each chapter's name.
- Use a one-word title for each chapter based on character names or places. Or maybe a color, descriptor, or an item that invokes imagery pertinent to the chapter's theme.

DON'T BE SHY—IT'S TIME FOR YOUR BIOGRAPHY!

Jamie hates talking about herself, so writing her biography felt akin to being asked up on stage. How do you know what's best to say about yourself in your author biography?

Check out a few other author bios for ideas. What catches your interest? Is there humor, or does the wording hint at the author's genre before it's stated? You can include education, accolades, other published works, where you live, family information like if you're married and how many children you have, and then a few interesting facts that might or might not pertain to your writing. If someone asked you to tell them something about yourself at a party, what would you say?

Keep your bio and short and sweet. If you're a bestseller or award winner, be sure to include those details. Most author bios are written in third person, which can be super weird at first, but you get used to it.

TO PEN NAME OR NOT TO PEN NAME

You might have heard the suggestion to write your books under a pen name. But is it a good idea for you? Why would someone want to publish under a pen name?

- **Same author, different genres.** Amazon creates author pages for each author, so some authors who write wildly different genres and want them to be seen separately for marketing purposes. Pen names allow this to be achieved without damaging the author's brand. If Stephen King started writing picture books for toddlers, everybody would be pretty confused.
- **Shhh...** Anonymity can be desirable for writers for a variety of different reasons. Some authors who write very different genres don't want readers to skip over their work due to association. For example, someone who writes political non-fiction might have a pen name for their middle-grade fiction. Or they might use a pen name for their erotic fiction to avoid possible damage to their social life or career.
- **Avoiding confusion.** If an author shares a name with someone famous or has a very common name, they might consider using a pen name to either not be mixed up with the famous person or to not be lost in the fray of other writers with the same name.
- **How do you spell that?** Some names are just difficult to remember, pronounce, or spell. Sometimes choosing a simpler

pen name is a marketing decision—word-of-mouth can be an author's best friend.

- **Gender issues.** Sadly, some genres are so associated with gender that people are more willing to read books in that genre by a certain gender. For example, some men write romances under a woman's pen name. We aren't saying this is necessary, but it is a reason some writers choose to do it. If you're wavering back and forth on this, we suggest you talk to other writers in your genre and see what works for them.

Do consider, if you end up writing books under two or more different names, you will also be faced with the decision to have to maintain separate Facebook pages, websites, blogs and author newsletters. It can be a ton of work, but might be worth it depending on the reasons.

CHOOSING CATEGORIES

Choosing a category, or genre, can be tricky. Especially if your book encompasses multiple genres like our books do.

We suggest starting broad and narrowing down from there. Here are some questions to help you get started with identifying your book's genre:

1. Fiction or non-fiction?
2. Does the story occur on Earth or another world?
3. Do the events take place in the past, present, or future?
4. Who is the target audience—and what is their age, gender, and/or interests?
5. What's the central type of conflict—internal or external?
6. If it's romance, what's the heat level? (Think of it in terms of movie ratings.)
7. What is the narrator's point of view—first person, second person, third person limited, or third person omniscient?

SETTING UP YOUR
AMAZON AUTHOR PAGE

Once your book is listed on Amazon—wait, can we just take a second to think about that? Your book will be listed on Amazon.com! Hurray!!!

Okay, sorry. Once your book is listed on Amazon, you will want to set up an Amazon author page using a website called Author Central. There are many great reasons to do this, and it's absolutely free.

- **Readers will be able to find** all your books in the same place.
- **You can post links** to your website and more author info.
- **Readers can choose to 'follow' your Amazon page.** When you release a new book, they will receive an automated e-mail announcement from Amazon.
- **You can check several statistics,** such as your author rank, new reviews, and your book's sales rank over time.
- **Insert your blog's RSS feed** (consult your individual blog's help section to figure out how to do this for your website) for your blog posts to automatically show on your Amazon Author Page when you add them to your blog.

To get started on your Author Central page, go to AuthorCentral.Amazon.com and follow the very simple, step-by-step instructions.

Check out other books on Amazon you would consider to be in your book's category and use them for reference. If you're still in doubt, ask other authors what they think your book would be best classified as. The Amazon KDP forums and Kboards are both good places to post for advice.

KEYWORDS & TAGS

Keywords are extremely important, because they are what readers use to search for books they want to read. Entire books have been written on this subject, and of course this will vary by genre like everything else, but we'll do our best to point you in the right direction for a solid start. Authors and publishers change keywords on their books all the time to find out which ones perform the best, so it's a constant evolution to find the right niche and gain exposure to the right audiences.

So don't stress too much over your first selection of tags—you should be doing a good deal of juggling over time to experiment and find what works best for your book. To start, we suggest using the same methods as you'd use to determine your book's categories: check similar books to yours.

The trick is to find out what words people are using to search for and find books like yours. They should be very specific to what makes your book unique, so you'll have the best chance of landing a sale when their search connects with your book page.

You may only use seven keywords when you create your Kindle book, so choose wisely. Don't worry about words that are obvious, like 'novel,' 'Kindle,' and 'book.' If you're writing a supernatural thriller, words like 'angels,' 'apocalypse,' and 'vampires' will probably serve you better by being specific to what your book offers—and what your readers are searching for.

TOOLS TO HELP FIND GREAT KEYWORDS

1. **Kindle Keyword Analyzer.** This free tool is great for discovering words that more Amazon customers are searching for: https://moopato.com/kindle-analyzer Type in your book's genre and take a look at the top sellers. Are romances in the top? Mail-order brides? Amish fiction? Drill down on niche keywords to make sure you are reaching an optimum audience.

   But be truthful. If you include keywords that misrepresent your book, you will not only wind up with angry customers, but you'll also risk your distributor's wrath. For example, if you use keywords for romantic suspense for your how-to book on gardening, Amazon probably won't let it fly.

2. **KDP Rocket.** This is an expensive tool up front (about $100), but if you're a veteran indie publisher who can use it for multiple books over time, it can save you a lot of time. Simply enter your competitor's book tiles, author names, genres, or concepts and it will generate a long list of possible keywords for you. Pretty nifty! https://kdprocket.com

3. **Amazon Marketing Services (AMS).** This is actually an advanced marketing tool, but it gives you crystal-clear data on which keywords perform the best for your book. There are a lot of technical ins and outs of navigating AMS and making it work for you, but once it does, it can be a very profitable method of marketing—and finding excellent keywords with experimentation.

   For more information on AMS, and the best strategies that have worked for us, check out *The Busy Mom's Guide to Novel Marketing.*

A FEW THOUGHTS ON BOOK DESCRIPTIONS/BACK COVER COPY

Writers have fits trying to write blurbs, and it's understandable. How do you summarize a book that has taken you months or even years to write?

The first step we suggest is to take a look at the most popular books in your genre (or the closest thing you can find if your book is multi-genre). What catches your eye about the blurb? What line (if any) attracts you the most?

There are specialists who can be hired to write your back cover copy and entire how-to books written on this one subject, so we won't pretend to be specialists. But a good place to start is thinking about your book's central conflict, so the reader will have a good idea of what they're getting into (and write positive reviews when you deliver on that promise). What makes your main character or setting unique? Don't be afraid to give away minor spoilers to hook your prospective reader—especially something they'll find out within the first few chapters, like the inciting incident (the spark that sets the story off).

Some people use a formula to write their blurbs, while some let the ideas flow organically. We recommend you ask your critique group or beta readers to look over your blurb and help to streamline it and make it more interesting. It can take many rounds of precise edits, but a blurb that really shines is worth the effort.

It's important your blurb be accurate. Readers *will* purchase a book based on the blurb, and if the book doesn't deliver, angry reviews will follow. For example, if you have a crime drama with a small romantic thread, don't advertise it as romantic comedy. Even if it has some elements of comedy and some romance, that's not your target audience. Lean heavily on your main genre in your description, but feel free to mention smaller elements, such as humor, romance, horror, faith-based, etc. Highlight what makes your book unique while staying true to your genre, and the sales will follow.

QUESTIONS

1. Who would you like to thank for help with your book? Make a list so you don't forget anyone. Do you have someone you want to dedicate your book to?
2. Should your book have a prologue? Is it necessary or could you fold that information into the first few chapters without compromising a good pace?
3. What genre/categories does your book fall into? Are there niche categories you could put it into that might reach a more specific audience?

Chapter 8

NOT-FOR-PROFIT BOOKS

"But when people say, 'Did you always want to be a writer?' I have to say no! I always was a writer."

— Thomas Merton

If you have purchased this book to find inexpensive ways to create books for special projects such as memoirs or family records, you've come to the right chapter. You may have a bedtime story you made up for your children at night or a tale your grandmother told you that you don't want to lose.

In this case, creating a book can be extremely affordable. It just takes a little time and effort to put together an heirloom that will grace the family shelf for years to come.

SO, WHEN'S YOUR NEXT CONCERT?

If we hear that someone is a guitar player, we don't ask them when their next concert will be. Nor do we expect everyone who paints to open a gallery. So why do people assume that everyone who writes should pursue publishing?

There's nothing wrong with being a hobby writer, or with creating a book and not publishing it for sale. And there's no reason to dump hundreds or even thousands of dollars into a book that will not recoup its own production cost.

KNOWING THE DIFFERENCE

Obviously, a few authors have written personal memoirs and published diaries that have sold millions of copies (Laura Ingalls Wilder, anyone?), but Amazon is flooded with personal memoirs that really should have been kept in the family. A historical account of whose grandma was whose may not be the most riveting tale to the general reader. But it can be a wonderful story to pass on for future generations.

If you're not looking to make a full-time career out of your writing—your own small business—then it's best not to release your book for purchase. Your book will not automatically sell itself… we guarantee it. Making money from indie book sales requires an upfront investment for producing a quality product, and then a constant, well-strategized investment into marketing.

> "Your book will not automatically sell itself… we guarantee it."

Please don't make a book as cheaply as possible and put it up for sale, assuming you'll somehow make millions without any marketing. It's this line of thinking that has lead to an overwhelmingly flooded marketplace and given people the idea that indie books are subpar.

CREATING AN AFFORDABLE NOT-FOR-PROFIT BOOK

TIPS FOR MAKING YOUR OWN COVER

In Chapter 3 we went over rules that every indie who plans on selling books to the general public should follow. But if you're producing a book for personal use, obviously you can use any cover you like. Of course, if you are creating a lasting family heirloom, you still want to make it look nice. So here are some tips:

- Choose a picture that best captures the spirit of your book. If you're putting together a book of memories about a family member, for instance, try to choose a candid photo rather than a formal pose.

- If at all possible, use a digital file that has been uploaded directly. Enhance the photo in a photo editing program and check for focus, clarity, and background noise. Ensure that your photo is high resolution—if it's too small (72 DPI or less than 1,000 pixels wide), it will look blurry when printed.

- If you must use a scanned photograph, take your photo to a business that offers copy/print services and have them scan it for you. Most of the time a professional machine will do a much better job.

- If you only have one photo and it has some blemishes, consider taking it to a professional photo editor for restoration. Make sure you check out their portfolio before shelling out any money.

- Instead of using an overused-to-death font that's standard on your computer, choose one or two custom fonts from a free website like fonts.google.com. Select one stylized font for your title and make it large on your cover, then pick a simpler serif or sans-serif font for your name or any other needed text. Ask for people's honest opinions before you decide it's ready.

SHOULD I GET MY BOOK EDITED EVEN IF I'M NOT PLANNING TO SELL IT?

Yes. Even if you don't hire a professional editor, find a few friends or family members who are grammatically inclined. They can go over your manuscript with you to check for those pesky typos. You'll be glad you did.

CRAZY CHEAP PAPERBACKS

The print-on-demand printer, CreateSpace, is our recommendation for most books for non-profit projects. It's easy to use, it doesn't take long to put together a decent book, and you pay the same low cost per book whether you order one paperback or one hundred. And if you use their Microsoft Word templates for formatting, you can create a paperback book without any cost besides the cost of printing (normally less than $10 per copy) for *free* aside from whatever you decide to spend on your cover. Feel free to use one of their ISBNs to avoid that unnecessary cost.

Please note: CreateSpace does not produce hardcover books. Book Baby is another site that *will* print hardcover books for you, but their prices are a quite a bit higher. Check out Chapter 4 for more information about formatting a book with CreateSpace.

POINTERS FOR COMMON TYPES OF NOT-FOR-PROFIT BOOKS

CHILDREN'S PICTURE BOOKS

Unless you have extensive experience with book formatting and graphic design, we suggest Book Baby for children's picture books and illustrated books. Their program is much more user-friendly for complicated projects like these, but it will have a cost. You can use CreateSpace for picture books, but they only offer paperback copies and you'll have to figure out everything yourself.

If you are uploading drawings or paintings, scan the pictures carefully and check them in a photo program for clarity before including them in a file. Make sure all pencil marks and eraser scuffs are blended out with a photo-editing program.

FAMILY MEMORIES

Family photographs make great additions to memoirs, especially for family members. But make sure you get permission from the person in the photograph before including the photo in your book. Even if you're not making a profit on your project, it's a nice thing to do (and it'll make Thanksgiving less awkward).

You have two choices to upload old photographs: you can scan them or take pictures of them. If you don't have a quality scanner, you might consider taking them to a professional copy/print business like Staples or even a photo lab to make sure the quality is the best it can be. Some of these places can even restore photos to remove blemishes such as water damage and creasing, but keep in mind this can get pricey.

If you decide to include color photographs inside your book, CreateSpace will charge the price for a full-color book, even if only a few pages have color photographs. But your front and back cover can be in color with no extra charge.

COOKBOOKS

Personal cookbooks loaded with family recipes make wonderful family gifts and can be great fundraisers for churches and other organizations. There are several sites, like createmycookbook.com, dedicated to helping you create spiral-bound, quality cookbooks for a reasonable price.

ARTISTIC PORTFOLIOS & PHOTO BOOKS

If you are a photographer and want to show off your art, as a portfolio or otherwise, we recommend you do research to find the best portfolio producer. The printers we have listed in this book are designed more for inexpensively-produced paperbacks for the masses.

Or if you want to put together a book with family photos or perhaps a photo journal, we recommend Shutterfly. They have easy to use templates and are reasonably priced.

QUESTIONS

1. How much do you plan on spending to produce your not-for-profit book? How many copies do you want, and how much do you estimate the printing cost will be?
2. What is the main purpose for your not-for-profit book? Can your goals be accomplished regardless of cost, or would it be worth a small investment to have a higher quality cover, editing, or formatting?
3. Do you need a hardcover and/or ebook version, or will a paperback suffice?

Chapter 9

PRE-MARKETING:
PREPARING FOR LAUNCH

"Good marketing helps a bad product fail faster."

— Thomas Umstattd Jr., CEO of Author Media

Now that you have this amazing book all ready, you'd like to actually sell it, right? You upload the final, proof-read-to-death Kindle file, wait breathlessly for Amazon to approve it, and the next day, when you search for the book's title—POOF!—it's there. You're an author!

You scream, jump up and down, and call your best friend. You break out the last precious pieces of Halloween candy you've been hoarding away for a special occasion.

Running to your Kindle account at kdp.amazon.com, you click the 'Reports' tab in breathless anticipation. Now, you don't want to get *too* excited. But hey, you worked really hard, right? Your book is awesome! You've poured your heart, soul, and money into this project for months, maybe years. But you can't expect too much. Probably only fifty or sixty sales in the first hour.

The bar graph flashes on screen and your heart drops. Flatline.

No sales? How can that be? Maybe it takes time for the data to show up, right?

Hours pass. Then an entire day. Still no sales. Your BFF promises she'll download 'after I get back from my cruise.'

Was all your effort in vain? Does *anyone* want to read your book?

Calm down. Don't panic. This doesn't have to happen to you. There are steps you can take months before your book goes live on Amazon to make sure you have plenty of sales on your first day and beyond.

Please keep in mind, we are only dusting over the basics of pre-launch marketing in this chapter. You can find many more of our very best marketing secrets in our third book in this series, *The Busy Mom's Guide to Novel Marketing*. Marketing is a subject very near and dear to our hearts. But we know that for some people, the very idea makes their eyes glaze over. So we've broken it down into simple steps so you can learn as you go. Ready to dive in?

A NOTE ON TIME AND MONEY

If you're a busy mom, you have already made sacrifices to write, edit, and produce your book. So it may seem impossible to devote any time to marketing. But if you want your book to sell, you *must* market it. We suggest carving out at least 2-3 hours per week (at the very least) to set up promotional opportunities for your books. Marketing is like cookie dough: you only get out what you put into it.

You will also find that many promotional services (email newsletters or websites such as BookBub, Freebooksy, or Robin Reads—there's more info about these in book 3) come with a hefty cost. This does *not* always work on the cookie dough principle. Some thousand-dollar services won't get you a single sale. Before you sink a penny into any type of promotion, make sure you ask other authors *in your genre* how they've done with the same promotional site or method.

THE PROMO SITE SLEUTH

Besides checking with other authors on how a particular promo site does for your genre, there's another way you can get a rough idea of how your book might do. Since promotions generally start in the morning and take a bit of time during the day to generate sales, we suggest you do this check in the evening:

Go to the promo site you're interested in and find the book that's closest to your genre. Be as specific as possible (for instance, don't check a steamy romance if yours is squeaky clean). Click on the book's Amazon listing and scroll down to see where it's ranked. If it's in the top 10 of its Amazon category and in at least the top 5,000 in the Amazon store overall, then your book will probably do well on that promotional site.

If the book you're comparing is on a free promo, make sure you check the 'free' section in its category on Amazon. This book should be in the top 5 of its category and in the top 1,000 of Amazon's free books section. If this isn't the case, we don't suggest you try the site.

If Jamie and Angela had done this when they were just starting out, they would have saved hundreds, if not thousands, of dollars over time trying to figure out what worked for their books. We're just sayin'.

Always keep track of when you have the promotion, what site, and which book you promoted. Go back afterwards to make a note of how many sales, free downloads, and/or KENP (Kindle Unlimited) pages read. If you are like us and forget what we had for breakfast by lunch time, you'll be glad you wrote it down.

PRE-LAUNCH MARKETING

Remember that marketing platform we mentioned earlier? Months before your book is published, you should be working on gathering a fan base. Here are some ways to get that started:

1. **Pre-orders.** As soon as you have a certain date for when your book will be ready (cover, formatting, editing—everything), add a few weeks to that and then set up an Amazon Kindle pre-order. Basically, Amazon will set up a listing with your cover and book info so that readers can pay for the book right away. As soon as the date arrives, the Kindle book will be delivered to their device.

But *please be careful.* Give yourself a couple weeks of padding for emergencies—the busy mom life is never dull. And if you set up a pre-order and don't deliver when you promise, Amazon will prevent you for setting up a pre-order again for an *entire* year.*

2. **Social media and email newsletters.** Post updates on your blog and/or in your monthly newsletter. Did you go somewhere interesting to gather information for your book? Take pictures! Share fascinating facts about the place you visited. Did you interview someone? Ask for their permission to share a few quotes from the interview.

Even if you are writing science fiction or fantasy, chances are you'll have to do some kind of research. Offer a compelling tidbit about a fighting style or the history of a weapon. Share what piqued your interest, and chances are someone else will be interested too.

3. **Cover reveal.** Cover reveals should be done 2-4 weeks before your book goes on sale. People might be so interested in the cover they'll immediately want to pre-order the book so they won't forget to buy it!

4. **Ask other authors or editorial review sites for endorsements.** If you're friends with any authors in your genre—especially authors with large audiences—humbly ask them for a possible endorsement of your

book. Be sure to give them plenty of time to read, and be thankful no matter what they say. If you land a few positive endorsements, you can list them in the front of your book and/or pick one to put on the cover. You could also consider paying an arm and a leg for an editorial review from Kirkus Reviews, Publisher's Weekly, or Library Journal (or Readers' Favorite for free)—just realize that it won't necessarily be a *good* review.

5. **ARC giveaways.** Submit ARCs (advanced reader copies) of your book to readaholics and bloggers to garner reviews and interest before your book is released. There are hundreds of people out there who love to review books in exchange for free reading material. Ask them to leave *honest* reviews on or before launch day on your book's Amazon, Goodreads, and/or Barnes & Noble pages. You can remind them with a kind email on launch day, and don't forget to reiterate that your ARC copy was not the final version.

But be careful. Make sure you respectfully ask the blogger if they are willing to do a review (and what format they prefer) before you send them a copy. Also, many reviewers are willing to read digital copies now, so you don't always need to send a costly paperback copy. Don't be offended if a blogger declines; many bloggers have huge backlogs with months of reading lists filled. Keep trying, though—you never know when you'll catch someone's attention!

6. **Host a blog tour.** Although this isn't necessary, organizing a blog tour can be a cheap way to spread the word about your book launch. Find several bloggers interested in your genre and ask them if they'd be willing to post an honest review on their blog (and hopefully Amazon and Goodreads as well) in exchange for a free copy of your book. If you're offering other goodies as well, like an exclusive giveaway, bloggers enjoy doting upon their audience. It can be an easy way to fill their blogging schedule and a lot of collective fun.

To organize your own tour, find 7-14 bloggers and plan out a schedule so each person posts on a different day during the tour's one- or two-week time period. Create special blog tour graphics for the bloggers to include in their post and allow them to interview you. Or if you don't want to organize it all yourself, there are plenty of organizers out there who are already friends with lots of bloggers. The cost for this generally hovers around $50.

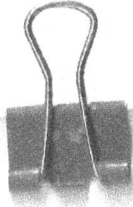

ALL ABOARD THE PRE-ORDER TRAIN!
RELEASING A SERIES ALL AT ONCE

If you are a superhero amazing mom writer and have the time and patience for this strategy, it can reap great rewards.

Many authors use these fabled things called 'Amazon algorithms.' These involve strategies and math--two things Angela tries to avoid like the plague, but she also likes to sell books, so there's that.

Some authors will write and prepare an entire series (or at least the first two books) before they launch the first book. They plan the launch of the second book in the series 30-60 days after the first book's launch.

Supposedly, this causes the series to catch on to these fabled Amazon algorithms and keep perpetuating the series, generating more sales. If you'd like to read more about this, check out Chris Fox's excellent book Launch to Market. He does a much better job of explaining this than we do. (Hey, we're writers, not mathematicians.)

REVIEWS

Your book's reviews are one of the most important factors to its long-term success. It's great to have plenty of reviews on all kinds of websites—from Goodreads to Barnes & Noble to Books-A-Million—but positive reviews will do you the most good on Amazon.com.

Amazon doesn't allow Kindle reviews on a book until its launch date, but a way to get around this policy is to release your paperback book a few days before your Kindle book (trust us, very few people will notice). Amazon will automatically link up your paperback page and Kindle page, so reviews on the paperback edition will also populate on your Kindle page. Then send an email to your beta readers, ARC reviewers, or your street team to remind them to post their honest reviews on launch day.

Please don't pay anyone *anything* for five-star reviews! It's against Amazon's Terms of Service to compensate someone directly—other than offering a free sample—to review your product. However, you can pay a matchmaking service that will hook you up with readers willing to leave *honest* reviews in exchange a free copy of your book. More details on this below in the 'A Few Ways to Get Reviews' section—just be careful. You don't want to get banned from Amazon. They will find you. In the dark. With a bulldozer. Okay, maybe not, but still.

Unfortunately, if you have a bunch of friends and family who leave you reviews, Amazon is very likely to remove them. And they could possibly shut down your listing as well if too many of these pop up.

So what you need are organic reviews from readers Amazon can't tie to you in any way (and believe us—they have their ways). For example, if you trade reviews with another writer, Amazon could also figure out you traded and again, might remove *both* of your reviews, even if they aren't five-star ones. Amazon also has a habit of removing reviews for mysterious reasons us mere mortals cannot grasp. Sometimes in big batches that leave us all reeling, but we digress.

Please don't take this information as an indication reviews are a waste of time to gather. They are very important for several reasons, and these are the top two:

1. **Readers pay attention to reviews.** Just like any other consumer product, readers will check out reviews to see what everyone else thinks of the book. Not only will they be checking the average rating and the amount of reviews, they'll also be looking for content information, like if the book was well written and kept reader's attention. Or if it made them cry happy tears or hide under the covers or burn the book in a custom-crafted bonfire.

    People looking for clean reads will check for content advisories, while readers desiring steamy content will see if the story is hot enough for them. This is one reason why we can't stress enough the importance of making sure your content description, tags, and Amazon blurb match the content of your book. Do *not* try to fool your readers into buying a book that isn't what they want. They will deliver their wrath in your book's reviews.

2. **Promo sites require reviews.** Most promotional sites worth their salt will require your book have a certain number of reviews and a certain positive percentage rating. Some require as few as 5 while a few require 35 - 50. That can seem like a daunting number, but if you work diligently to get your book out there, it will happen naturally over time.

A FEW WAYS TO GET REVIEWS

Word of mouth. Consider your audience. Is your book for young adults? Children? Veterans? Soccer moms? Find a group of these folks and ask if they will read and review your book. Book clubs still exist, and they're awesome. So are activity centers, libraries, and religious groups.

You can order paperbacks for them to review from your printer or see if they will accept a digital copy. Most people can pull up a Word Document or PDF file and read it on their phone just like a Kindle book. Ask them to mention that they received the book for free in exchange for their honest review.

Facebook groups. Whatever genre your book is in, there are probably several Facebook groups devoted to avid readers of that type of story. Many of them will allow you to post a link to your book and offer free copies for honest reviews. Be sure to check the rules of each particular group before you do this.

Goodreads. Goodreads hosts giveaways where you can offer your books as prizes. You can offer as many paperback books or ebooks as you want, but the contest itself is *expensive*. We've generally seen a few hundred to a few thousand entrants per giveaway, but it can vary depending on genre (as everything does). We've generally seen a 1:4 ratio for reviews given to books won. So while this can be an effective way to get reviews, it's also not a sure thing. And did we mention it's expensive?

Here's a cheaper option: Goodreads also has specific groups of people who like to get free books in exchange for reviews. This is perfectly fine according to Amazon's Terms of Service, however, the reader *must* say they are giving an honest review in exchange for a free book.

Request reviews from readers. Seems simple, right? Place a note at the end of your paperbacks and ebooks asking for an honest review. When you sell a book to someone at a book signing, tell them you'd love to hear their honest thoughts in an Amazon.com review.

Paid review matchmakers. You must be *extremely* careful when advancing in this territory. You should *never* pay someone for a review on Amazon—it's against Amazon's Terms of Service and could land you in serious trouble.

But there are legitimate companies—such as NetGalley, Story Cartel, eBook Discovery's Read & Review program, and Authors Cross Promotion—who offer your book to people in the *hopes* that they will leave a review. You are paying for them to present your book to this audience of reviewers, and nothing else. There are other options like these available that are perfectly fine according to Amazon's Terms of

Service, but please just do your homework before using them.

Beware the very expensive NetGalley. While they can generate a large amount of reviews for you, their reviewers are notorious for being overly critical and even vicious.

Editorial reviews. Some services, such as Kirkus Reviews, Publisher's Weekly, Library Journal, and Readers' Favorite, will charge for giving your book one honest review. You can use these for listing in the front of your book, the Editorial Reviews section on your Amazon book page, or choose the snazziest one to put on your cover.

With the exception of Readers' Favorite (which is free unless you pay them to do it quickly), these sites tend to be very expensive. They promise an in-depth, honest review and publish the review on their website or in a periodical. They are not actual Amazon reviews for your book's product page.

Please note: a paid review doesn't necessarily mean a *good* review. We know some folks who have been reamed by Kirkus and Publisher's Weekly.

MARKETING TO THE GREAT BEYOND

Since the third book in this series is devoted to this subject—check out *The Busy Mom's Guide to Novel Marketing* for far more detail—we'll give just a few suggestions for getting your marketing off the ground.

1. **Facebook groups.** Read the rules and follow them, since not all groups allow promotional posts and some are restrictive about content/genre. We suggest you join 10-20 groups in your genre and post links to your books regularly, especially when your book is newly released and/or on sale. It's better to be an active voice in the community rather than sound like a robot who only posts about your own books. Nobody likes bots.

2. **Paid promotional websites.** Promotional websites for books tend to have email newsletters with tens of thousands of rabid readers chomping at the bit for the next book deal. You can pay them a fee to have your book included in their email newsletter, on their social media, or on a post on their website. We love combining our favorite promotional sites with our own 'free-pulsing' strategy, and we discuss this in detail along with a list of our favorite promotional sites in *The Busy Mom's Guide to Novel Marketing.* Many sites aren't worth their price and some are flat-out snakes, so beware.

3. **AMS ads and Facebook advertising.** There are all kinds of websites that will post ads of your books for a fee—normally a few cents for each time someone clicks on your ad. These can be tricky to make a profit, but very lucrative once you've got it down. Sites we recommend checking out include AMS (Amazon Marketing Services), Facebook, and BookBub advertising. This is a pretty advanced technique, so do plenty of research before spending your hard-earned moolah on advertising.

4. **Forums.** Kboards and Scribophile are places that allow limited sharing of books you have written, and there are countless forums dedicated to specific genres of books that are happy to allow sharing. Again, read the terms and conditions carefully.

5. **Local events.** Book signings, craft fairs, coffee houses, and local bookshops are great places to get out there and share your book and meet readers. Never be afraid to ask for a table or booth!

6. **Newsletter swaps.** Make friends with other authors in your same genre and do a "swap" with their blog and/or newsletter. You will write a blog post about your books for their audience, and you feature them to your own audience. Win-win!

QUESTIONS

1. How much time can I devote to marketing each week, and when would be the best days?
2. Which methods can I use first to start gathering reviews?
3. How much money do I want to devote to marketing? What percentage of earnings will I put back into marketing once my books are established?

Chapter 10

MARKETING PLATFORMS:
FOUNDATIONS FOR YOUR INDIE CAREER

"Very simply, a platform is the thing you stand on to get heard. It's your stage. But unlike a stage in a theatre, today's platform is not built of wood or concrete or perched on a grassy hill. Today's platform is built of people. Contacts. Connections. Followers."

— Mike Hyatt

When Angela first decided to self-publish her book, it never occurred to her that she would need to build a fanbase for her books. She figured she could just put a book out there on Amazon, and people would hopefully see the cover, like it, and buy it.

For a very few people, this is the case. Sometimes a writer will come up with just the perfect niche product and keywords, post their story up, and WHAM-O, the sales will come rolling in.

But... we're only saying this because you might actually meet one of these legendary authors one day and get mad because we said no one can ever do this. It does happen—people win the lottery and American Idol, too. It's extraordinarily rare.

So let's move on with real life and take your best realistic shot at becoming a career writer, shall we?

BASE BUILDING: PLACES TO SET UP YOUR PLATFORM

Most authors, if they want to make sales, have to build something called a marketing 'platform.' This is different from a distribution or sales platform like Amazon or CreateSpace—your marketing platform is basically a network of enthusiastic fans who love your books and will buy your newest release as soon as it comes out.

Your platform is far more important than any single marketing campaign. It is a slow and steady build that will make each of your book launches more successful than the last—the catalyst that will transform your writing into a career with predictable, dependable income.

Now, you may think that since this is your first book, building a platform isn't important, but it is. We will explore a few ways you can get started—there are many great ideas out there.

YOUR AUTHOR WEBSITE & BLOG

Your author website is home base for your marketing platforms, from social media to your email newsletter to your blog. Like a digital business card, your website lets authors connect with you wherever you're available, and it should provide plenty of juicy information about your books and clear direction where to buy them.

Blogs may seem old-fashioned, but they're still a great way to reach readers, and you can post to them as many or few times as you like—

though consistency is a key to organic growth—so they're a nice option for busy moms. Cover reveals, author interviews, reviews of books in similar genres, and posts about life observations are all worthy content for a blog. Readers love stories that help them connect to an author, so you could share a story about your child and how they inspired your writing, or something about being a mom. Or how your attempt at chicken fettuccine alfredo became a call-the-fire-department situation.

Content is key—post about not what's interesting to you, necessarily, but to your target audience. If you are writing historical fiction, for instance, you might consider including articles about characters in history from that time period. Include recipes and interesting facts about inventions and practices during a specific era. If you write romances, you could include articles for date ideas and lists of romantic cities and/or countries. Get creative!

If you'd like to beef up your blog and don't have time to write lengthy articles, consider adding a photo journal of a day trip. Swap author interviews with another writer of a similar genre. Or swap complete articles that both you and another author can use. You'll essentially be marketing to each other's audiences for free. Sweet!

SETTING UP YOUR WEBSITE: FREE VS CUSTOM

Some writers choose to purchase a domain name and hire a designer to build a custom website while others opt for a free website. How do you know which option is best for you?

FREE WEBSITES:

- **They're free!** A simple, free way to get started in a jiffy. Did we mention they're free?
- **Easy to use.** Clean web interfaces on most blog sites like

Wordpress, Blogger, and Weebly are intuitive enough for even non-techies to set up and manage their own website.

- **Not-super-professional website address.** The web host's name will be included as part of your web address. For example, Angela's free website is angelacastillowrites.weebly.com, while Jamie's custom site is jamiesfoley.com. However, some sites like Wordpress.com will let you use your own paid domain name to mask the address.
- **Stuck in template land.** Free websites are restricted to themes, so design and functionality is limited.
- **No control over ads.** The web host may display their own ads on your website outside of your control, and you might not be able to host your own ads.

CUSTOM-BUILT WEBSITES:

- **Super professional website address & emails.** You can choose your own domain name, such as jamiesfoley.com (we recommend using your author name if you can). Domain names cost about $12-$15 per year. You can also get your own email address at your domain, such as jamie@jamiesfoley.com.
- **Unlimited design, but costly hosting.** You can design your site however you like—you're only limited by your imagination and your webmaster's ability. However, the cost of your own web hosting (which is different from your domain name) runs about $115-$130 per year. On top of that, your web designer will charge their own fee, which could run anywhere from a couple hundred to a few thousand depending on their experience. You might also have to pay a monthly fee for your website's maintenance if you don't know how to do it yourself. Ask your webmaster to teach you how to maintain your own website to save a lot of money over time. They'll still be there to bail you out when you need help.
- **A source of revenue.** You can monetize your website by signing

up for programs like Google Adsense to display ads on your website. You can also sign up for referral programs like Amazon Associates, which pays you a small percentage of purchases on Amazon to you when links on your website refer the buyer.

Most free websites will do just fine for authors who are just getting started, but you might want to upgrade later on in your career. Or you might find that your money is better spent on marketing campaigns or your daughter's gymnastics lessons.

As a professional web designer, Jamie only recommends that writers pay for snazzy custom websites if they're very serious about going for a contract with a traditional publisher or their career is established enough to warrant a crazy-awesome website—and afford it with ease.

SOCIAL MEDIA

Facebook isn't the only social media site you could be on, but you shouldn't feel pressured to join every single social website out there. Choose one or two that you enjoy and will be consistent with. We do recommend that Facebook be one of those, but the best choices for you depend on where your readership is.

- **Facebook:** The largest social media platform where just about everyone is. Nowadays it's hard to have your posts actually seen without paying Facebook to promote them, but it's still worth it to set up a free page under your author name.
- **Twitter:** A decently large site, but not as big as people make it out to be. You'll do great on Twitter if you share things that are funny, inspirational, or news-oriented.
- **Pinterest:** Bloggers love Pinterest, and for good reason. It's an image-based site that links directly back to the original post—on the blogger's website. This site is used mostly by women around age 20-40.

- **Instagram:** This image-driven social media site is great for photographers and artists. Book lovers have their own popular hashtag here—#bookstagram. If you enjoy imagery and love snapping beautiful pics, this is the platform for you.
- **Snapchat:** Selfie central. Used mostly by teenagers and young adults. Not the best for marketing your books, but we suppose it's plausible. At least it's a way for readers to connect with their favorite authors.

Authors have written entire books about social media advertising, and we will cover this subject more thoroughly in The Busy Mom's Guide to Novel Marketing. Facebook & Twitter ads have proven to be profitable for some, but they can also lose you a ton of money if you don't go into it with a proven strategy. And strategies always have to change, because technology, the internet, and the book industry are always changing.

"Just make sure you post relevant, interesting things at least every few days or so, and about five times as often as you post something promotional. Nobody wants to subscribe to a stream of constant ads."

GETTING STARTED ON FACEBOOK

The first thing you should do as an author is create a separate author page for yourself on Facebook—this is different from your profile. Unfortunately, it's against Facebook's policies to post promotions on profile pages. But you don't want to lose friends and annoy your family over your 'buy my book!' posts anyway, right?

We recommend naming it something pertaining to your writing (such as Suzie Someone, Author) instead of your book series. Why? Because you might write a different series or book someday, and you still want people to find you.

After you've created your public author page, invite any of your Facebook friends you think might be interested in getting info about your writing (not all of your friends and family and your brother-in-law's cousin's sister, Aunt Suzie Someone). Don't get your feelings hurt if not everyone wants to join your page. People are particular about their Facebook accounts.

You can post giveaways, new blog posts, cover reveals, and other book announcements to your new page. But just like with your blog, we suggest you post other interesting content as well. Maybe quotes from your books on pretty backgrounds, or anything you think your specific audience would find interesting. If you write young adult fiction, post funny memes. If you write in the Christian genres, post verses or inspirational quotes. If you write political commentary, post your thoughts on news stories. Just make sure you post relevant, interesting things at least every few days or so, and about five times as often as you post something promotional. Nobody wants to subscribe to a stream of constant ads.

EMAIL NEWSLETTERS

One of the first ways every author should begin building a platform is by setting up a newsletter. There are many ways to do this, but one of the easiest websites to use is called MailChimp. MailChimp is free to use until you hit 2,000 subscribers—after that they charge a monthly amount depending on how many subscribers you have.

Be very careful how you acquire subscribers. You want to make sure they are folks who will actually be interested in reading what you send, because you'll eventually be paying for them to remain on your list.

USING A CONTEST TO GARNER NEWSLETTER SIGN-UPS

One way to build your newsletter list is by holding relevant giveaways or contests for people who enjoy reading your book's genre. Amazon gift cards always work as enticing bait, and you might consider throwing in a paperback copy of your signed book as well. If you'd like to start building subscribers before your book is ready, consider offering a bestselling book in your genre. We recommend you keep the total prize value between $25-$50.

WHAT SHOULD I PUT IN MY NEWSLETTER?

We don't recommend a big old ad, for starters. What would pique your interest? Contests, giveaways, and cover reveals are good ideas. We've also done photo essays, shared favorite book lists, and recipes. Share a picture of your child dressed as a character from your book, or a picture they've drawn of a fantastical beast from your epic fantasy. Always include links to your products somewhere in the newsletter.

Only send out one newsletter per month, at the most. Even if you have brilliant content, people will get annoyed if you send out too much.

Kind of like that friend on Facebook that shares a picture of every single meal, or every 'cute' thing their kid says.

HOW DO I GET PEOPLE TO SIGN UP FOR MY NEWSLETTER?

Here lies the tricky part—and the reason we suggest starting all of this now. It takes years to build up a strong newsletter following.

MailChimp provides several ways for you to share your sign-up link, including a link you can include in the back of your Kindle books. You can put a pop-up link on your website, blog post and Facebook page. Take a clipboard to gather email addresses at book signings and readings (always make sure people know they are signing up for a newsletter). Hand out your card with the link and include it in email correspondence.

USING A FREE SHORT STORY TO GARNER NEWSLETTER SIGN-UPS

The most solid long-term way to build your newsletter list is to offer a free short story or another piece of your writing in exchange for one's email address. You'll get plenty of sign-ups, and as a bonus, you'll probably get them hooked on your awesome series, which they'll gladly pay full price for!

BUILDING RELATIONSHIPS & SPREADING THE WORD

LOCAL BOOKSTORES

Most writers have a dream of waltzing into a local bookstore and seeing their book on the shelf, and this dream can be realized. In some cases, it's simply a matter of asking the owner if they will take your book on commission, but some places are more particular about what they accept. Just remember these steps:

Call before you go. Make sure they take books by local authors, and ask about the best time to come by. Some bookstores get slammed at certain times of the day and you don't want to be pitching your book through a long line of customers.

We suggest you don't say you're indie until you show them your book or unless they ask (don't lie). Sometimes indies have a reputation of not having well put-together products, and while most bookstore owners know there are many respected self-published authors, some have only seen the unprofessional side of the indie world. You want to be able to show them your polished, professional-looking book with its beautifully designed cover before they make a decision.

Be humble. You aren't the first local author to pitch your book, and you won't be the last. The book store owner has seen lots of books from people like you, and they probably will not be awed or impressed. What they will be, hopefully, is supportive and willing to help you out.

Be open. While a store might not agree to put your book on the shelf, they might be willing to let you plan or participate in a book signing. So don't get irritated if you don't get exactly what you asked for.

Be prepared. Don't expect to sell hundreds of books at every local event. If you drum up a good local fan base and announce when you will be delivering sequels to the shop, you might expect a handful of sales per year. But we still stress the importance of local presence. You never know when someone will pick your book for their book club and order twenty copies!

LIBRARIES

Donating your books to local libraries can be a great way to get your books out there, and people who read a book and enjoy it are likely to buy a copy for themselves (or the rest of the series).

But again, be humble. Some libraries don't accept self-published books. Make sure you hand the book directly to the librarian in charge of acquisitions, and make sure you are clear that you are a local author, donating the book to put in circulation. Otherwise, you might find it for sale in the library book shop.

Don't be surprised if the library declines the book. Some libraries have an across-the-board 'no indie' policy. It's sad but true.

Another thing to ask the librarian: some libraries host local author book talks and readings. They might be able to give you a slot on the calendar. If you have a children's book, you might also be able to schedule a story time. Make sure you always take your email sign-up clipboard to any of these events and ask people if they would like to receive your newsletter. If you use the magical word 'giveaway,' people are usually more willing to opt in.

BOOK FAIRS/EVENTS

Some authors swear by selling books at booths during local craft fairs and other events. This is especially effective if you are selling children's books or books of local interest, but we have seen success with all our genres, which span several different targeted groups. This is not only a good way to connect with local people who might be interested in having you come to do author talks or book signings, but it's also an excellent way to collect email addresses for your newsletter—especially if you have a gift card or small gift basket as a giveaway prize. (Again, always have it in writing that they will be receiving your newsletter if they enter.)

FORUMS

Online forums are great places to meet other indie authors and talk shop. Many of the tricks and tips we have learned over the years have been taught to us by patient and caring members of these types of forums. Some are new writers, while others have been in the practice for decades and are making 6 figures a year.

One good forum can be found in the 'community' section on the Kindle site, and another wonderful forum is called Kboards. Both of these communities are free to join, and they also allow you to list your books at the bottom of your signature so people can know where to find your writing.

QUESTIONS

1. What are some content ideas for my first newsletter?
2. Which social media websites would I be best at producing regular content for—and which would I enjoy the most?
3. Who would I contact at my local library to find out how to submit my books?

Thank you!

Whoa, you made it through! We know this book contained a *lot* of information on a *lot* of different topics, and that much of the subject matter is confusing or headache-inducing by nature. We hope that this book has been able to clarify some issues for you, and to steer you clear of problems we've slogged through during our own indie journeys.

So many details of publishing vary greatly depending on your passion for your genre, your goals, your place in life--there's no way we could write a one-size-fits-all book to perfectly address everyone's needs. A grandmother wanting to find an illustrator and produce a picture book for her grandchildren will have vastly different goals than a starry-eyed sci-fi writer with a hybrid career in her sights.

Whatever your case, we would love to connect with you to hear your story and address your specific needs. Track us down on the Busy Mom's website or Facebook page, or sign up for our email newsletter to keep an eye on what we're cooking up next. Our passion is helping writers just like you realize your dreams—no matter how epic they are.

Angela Castillo &
Jamie Foley

Sources

CHAPTER 2

CNBC: HERE'S NOW MANY AMERICANS ARE LIVING PAY-CHECK-TO-PAYCHECK

https://www.cnbc.com/2017/06/29/heres-how-many-americans-are-living-paycheck-to-paycheck.html

NEWSOK: FOUNDER, CEO OF TATE PUBLISHING ARRESTED ON EMBEZZLEMENT, EXTORTION CHARGES

http://newsok.com/article/5547934

CHAPTER 4

INGRAMSPARK BLOG: INGRAMSPARK VS CREATESPACE: RETURNABILITY

http://www.ingramspark.com/blog/ingramspark-vs-createspace

CHAPTER 5

AUTHOR EARNINGS: 55% OF ALL BOOKS SOLD IN 2017 WERE EBOOKS

http://authorearnings.com/report/january-2018-report-us-online-book-sales-q2-q4-2017

AUTHOR EARNINGS: 82% OF EBOOK SALES WERE ON THE KINDLE PLATFORM

http://authorearnings.com/report/february-2017

RETAIL DIVE: NOOK HAS LOST MORE THAN HALF ITS VALUE IN JUST OVER TWO YEARS

https://www.retaildive.com/news/barnes-noble-has-a-nook-problem/504554

CHAPTER 6

THE GOOD E-READER: THE HIGHEST GROWING SEGMENT OF PUBLISHING IS AUDIOBOOKS

https://goodereader.com/blog/digital-publishing/audiobook-trends-and-statistics-for-2017

STATISTA: SOME GENRES PERFORM BETTER IN AUDIOBOOK FORMAT THAN OTHERS

https://www.statista.com/statistics/249846/preferred-audiobook-genres-in-the-us

CHAPTER 9

AMAZON: KINDLE PRE-ORDER DETAILS AND THE PENALTY FOR MISSING DEADLINES

https://kdp.amazon.com/en_US/help/topic/G201499440

THE BUSY MOM'S GUIDE TO NOVEL MARKETING

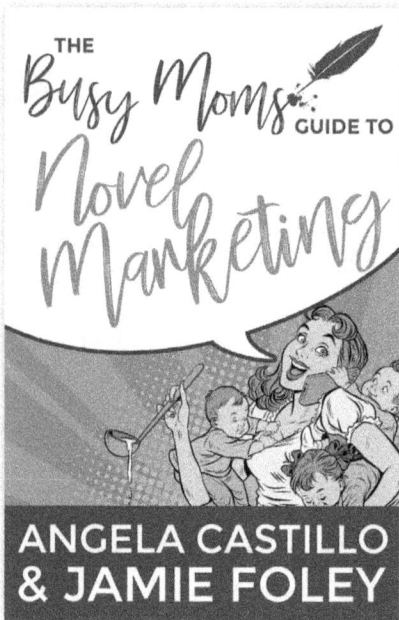

ANGELA CASTILLO & JAMIE FOLEY

Marketing your fiction novels can make you feel like a small fish in an ocean. How can you get your book to stand out from the crowd—and actually make money?

This guide is packed full of advice from career novelists Angela Castillo and Jamie Foley, including:

- Which paid promotions and ads actually work (and how to do them)
- How to build your email newsletter list and social media platforms
- Tips for book signings, booths, and events (and digital events, too)
- How to get your novels into bookstores & libraries
- Giveaway strategies that will sell novels faster than granny's hotcakes

THE BUSY MOM'S GUIDE TO WRITING

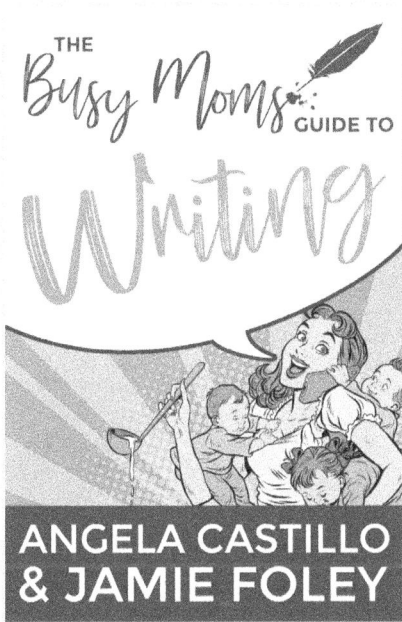

Are you a busy mom who loves to write, but doesn't know where to start? This easy-to-read guide by two bestselling, award-winning authors will help you make your writing dreams a reality.

From finding time to write, to showing you how to get your kids involved, this book will:

- Help you plan out your writing goals, time management, and financial budget
- Encourage you to enlist aid from the right people--critique partners, editors, cover designers, and more
- Guide you to making the best decision for you regarding independent and traditional publishing
- Give you questions to ask yourself at the end of each chapter to help you move closer to your writing dreams
- Steer you away from mistakes we've made

ANGELA CASTILLO & JAMIE FOLEY

ASK THE BUSY MOMS

your questions

& CHECK OUT THE PODCAST ON

PATREON

WWW.PATREON.COM/BUSYMOMBOOKS

Coming Soon!

SIGN UP FOR THE NEWSLETTER
FOR THIS EXCLUSIVE .PDF

50 Websites Every Author Should Know About: Angela and Jamie's 50 favorite websites that have helped them the most in their writing careers.

50 *websites*
EVERY AUTHOR
SHOULD KNOW ABOUT

ANGELA CASTILLO
& JAMIE FOLEY

free download!

WWW.BUSYMOMBOOKS.COM/NEWSLETTER

CONNECT WITH *Angela*

Angela Castillo has lived in Bastrop, Texas, home of the River Girl, almost her entire life. She studied Practical Theology at Christ for the Nations in Dallas. She lives in Bastrop with her husband and three children. Angela has written several short stories and books, including the Toby the Trilby series for kids.

WEBSITE
www.angelacastillowrites.weebly.com

FACEBOOK
www.facebook.com/adventurestobythetrilby

EMAIL NEWSLETTER
FREE BOOK WITH SIGN-UP!
http://eepurl.com/bLyYxb

AMAZON AUTHOR PAGE
www.amazon.com/Angela-Castillo/e/B00CJUELT0

CONNECT WITH *Jamie*

Jamie Foley loves strategy games, home-grown berries, and Texas winters. She's terrified of plot holes and red wasps.

Her husband is her manly cowboy astronaut muse. They live between Austin and the family cattle ranch, where their hyperactive spawnling and wolfpack can run free.

WEBSITE
www.jamiesfoley.com

FACEBOOK
www.facebook.com/jamiesfoley

EMAIL NEWSLETTER
FREE SHORT STORY FOR NEWSLETTER SUBSCRIBERS ONLY!
www.jamiesfoley.com/newsletter

AMAZON AUTHOR PAGE
www.amazon.com/Jamie-Foley/e/B00HJ8XIOQ

INSPIRING FICTION BY ANGELA CASTILLO

Texas Women of Spirit

Book 1: *The River Girl's Song*

Book 2: *The Comanche Girl's Prayer*

Book 3: *The Saloon Girl's Journey*

Bonus: *The River Girl's Christmas*

Toby the Trilby (children's series)

The Amazing Adventures of Toby the Trilby

The Further Adventures of Toby the Trilby

Toby the Trilby and the Forgotten City

Miss Main Street

Book 1: *Secondhand Secrets*

Book 2: *Blessed Arrangements*

Steampunk Fairy Tales
Multi-author short story collections

Volumes I, II, and III

Metal-Locks & Other Fairytales
A collection of eight short stories by Angela Castillo

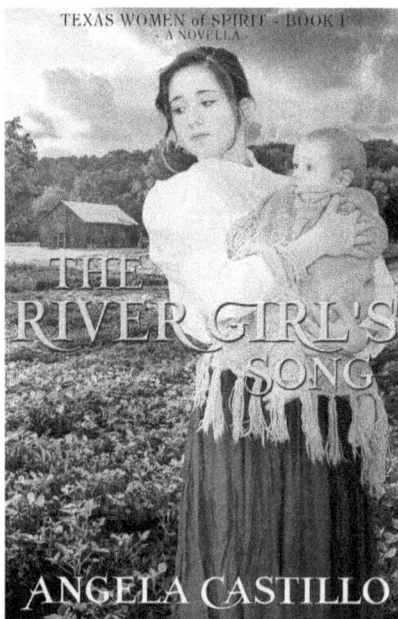

Zillia Bright never dreamed she'd be orphaned at sixteen and left to care for her baby brother and Papa's farm. With only a mule and a hundred-year-old shotgun, she must fight to protect what's hers.

Countless dangers lurk on the Bastrop Texas riverside. Zillia must rely on the help of her best friends, Soonie and Wylder, to hold her world together. With Zillia's struggles come unexpected miracles, and proof that God might just listen to the prayers of a river girl.

Clean, Christian fiction with a hint of romance.

THRILLING FICTION BY JAMIE FOLEY

The Sentinel Trilogy

Prequel novella: *Vanguard*

Book 1: *Sentinel*

Book 2: *Arbiter*

Book 3: *Sage*

Steampunk Fairy Tales
Multi-author short story collections

Volume III

*Coming soon: the **Emberhawk** series and the **Runes of Kona** series*

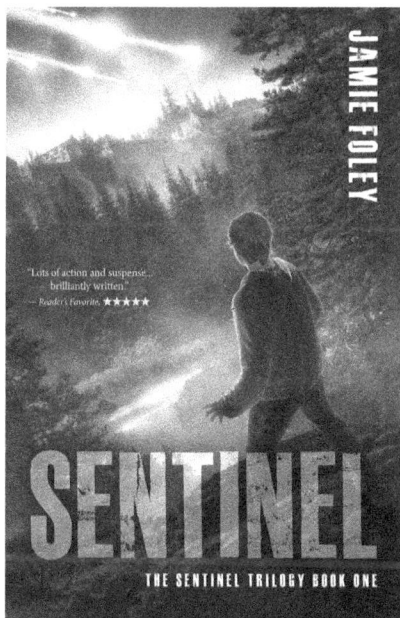

Blood-bonds with angels. Surreal mental abilities. Elemental gods.

The meteor storm wasn't such a big deal until a comet landed in the middle of the road. Now Darien's car is wrecked, his sister is bleeding out, and the only medical aid is at the reclusive Serran Academy.

Jet sees Darien for what he is: a lost teen who doesn't deserve to know about the aether gifts. And his sister's rare future-seeing ability is exactly what the enemy is after.

As fractured governments and shadow organizations vie for control of a dying world, the Serran Academy students—and their angelic secrets—are targeted for harvesting.

Clean young adult fantasy with fast-paced, epic adventure.

"Lots of action and suspense... brilliantly written."
— Reader's Favorite